The Book of Knowledge and Wonder

The Book of Knowledge
and Wonder

Dear Jerry,

it was great to see you and the
rest of the La Grange mafia in
Young Harris last week. Please
accept this book as a gift from one
writer to another. Best wishes

Steven Harvey

Ken Harvey

Judith Kitchen Select

OVENBIRD

Ovenbird Books, 2014
Port Townsend, WA

Dedication

For the women in my life: my mother who gave me the words, my grandmother who saved them for me, and my wife, Barbara, who listened and remembered until I was ready to hear.

in memoriam

Judith Kitchen

The Wonder of Knowledge:
An Introduction

"There is only one good. That is knowledge"—
Steven Harvey read those words as a child, leafing
through *The Book of Knowledge*, and he reads them again, in
the present, as he enters that same realm in search of a
mother who died when he was young. For most of his
adult life he simply deflected the nagging questions
surrounding her death. But sometimes we are given a gift.
In Harvey's case, a box of letters allows him the luxury of
speculation.

The letters give up their secrets long after the fact.
Harvey's entry into their world provides a clear example
of how past and present can be simultaneous. This book
chronicles a specific time in American history: a time
when new technologies opened doors for men, when they
could provide their families with a middle-class, suburban
life, and when their intelligent wives were often isolated
and lonely. At a time when a long-distance phone call was
reserved for serious crisis, the letter still reigned. Back and
forth, the words flew between daughter and mother—the
ordinary stuff of living: college, early marriage, babies,

and the growing feelings of inadequacy and (though it was not understood then as it is now) depression.

Watch the writer of nonfiction as he illuminates his craft. By asking himself the original "wonder questions" of his childhood, Harvey ignites a curiosity that takes him back into memory—but also allows him room for inference and imagination. By asking his current penetrating questions, he demonstrates how to probe the undersides of a lifetime. Harvey's self-conscious foray into his lost past exposes an intricate process of recovery: commenting on his own roving commentary, Harvey walks us through an experience even as he analyzes it, maintains distance even as he closes its gaps. Grief, yes, but grief in the wider context of knowing what a life can be, could have been. Stepping in and out of reminiscence and retrospection, Harvey begins to know his mother as an individual. In the end, he emerges with a kind of knowledge, to which he adds the well-earned word "wonder."

Judith Kitchen, October 2014

OVENBIRD

This book is published under the Judith Kitchen Select imprint of Ovenbird Books, a new publishing venture designed to bring literary nonfiction titles to the attention of the reading public. In the interest of quality and individuality, Judith Kitchen acts as editor and introduces each book; the writer has complete autonomy over content and design.

www: ovenbirdbooks.org

The Book of Knowledge and Wonder

In 1952, when I was three, my parents bought a set of *The Book of Knowledge,* ten hefty volumes bound in maroon leather each filled with questions from "The Department of Wonder." Like sentinels posted at the gates of wisdom, the books stood proudly on a shelf between the glossy forelocks of equestrian bookends, each volume embossed with a golden torch. It was, my mother explained in one of the hundreds of letters she wrote to my grandmother, a purchase as much for her as for her boy. "I have really been enjoying it. I've been studying the subjects of music and art so far," she explained. "That is how I've been spending some of my evening while Max is away." Reading *The Book of Knowledge* helped fend off the loneliness and depression that, sweeping over her during these years, eventually destroyed her.

The Book of Knowledge evolved from *The Children's Encyclopædia,* the inspiration of Arthur Mee, born to a working class family in Stapleford, England, whose formal education ended when he was fourteen. Questions posed by Mee's daughter Marjorie were the direct inspiration for the encyclopedia. In his letter "To Boys and Girls Everywhere" published in the first volume of

The Children's Encyclopædia, Mee writes that Marjorie's mind was filled with "the great wonder of the Earth. What does the world mean? And why am I here? Where are all the people who have been and gone? Where does the rose come from? Who holds the stars up? What is it that seems to talk to me when the world is dark and still?" Mee's wife had "thought and thought" about these questions "and answered this and answered that until she could answer no more. Oh for a book that will answer all the questions!" she complained. *The Children's Encyclopædia* was born.

What set his book apart, Mee explained, was the belief in children's eagerness for knowledge and their capacity for wonder. But he knew that his book also filled an important gap for adults. It "had the power to make plain to the average man, woman, and child the aspects and imports of the problems which the very men who had wrested them from nature could not make so plain." It offered up the mysteries of the few for the rest of us. By the time *The Children's Encyclopædia* had evolved into *The Book of Knowledge* it had added the "Department of Wonder" and each volume contained sections devoted to "wonder questions" like the ones Marjorie posed to her perplexed parents.

For my mother, who had dropped out of nursing school when she was nineteen to marry my father, the gaps in her education were becoming an embarrassment. Born Roberta Maxine Reinhardt, and called Bobbie, she had been the only child of her parents and beloved by the small Kansas town of Glen Elder where she grew up. Pretty and bright, she made nearly perfect grades but not without help. "As I remember I used to make A on every theme you wrote for me," she mentioned in one letter to my grandmother. A little unsure of herself when she entered nursing school in 1946, she created elaborate study schedules, but as she pursued her studies she became more confident. "I'm so thrilled about my subjects. There is an awfully lot of reading to do, but it is interesting." Anxieties about how hard the classes would be proved unfounded and she flourished in the program. "I've been wondering how I would like my nursing subjects—it is play to study them."

After marrying, that confidence in her abilities slowly eroded, especially when my father joined the pharmaceutical company American Cyanamid as a managing director and our young family moved from Dodge City, Kansas to Nanuet, New York, a suburb of the City. In the 1952 letter about buying *The Book of Knowledge*, she describes a lavish dinner party served by maids. "Of course the conversation got around to operas and plays," she complains, "as it always does here" and she did not feel comfortable again, she adds wryly, "until they all started talking about the pigs in Missouri." She admits that it was "an educational evening" and after it was over "a nice experience to have," but laments that she was caught off guard: "had I known beforehand I would have studied up." *The Book of Knowledge* was her way to "study up." "I've done very little brain work since I got out of school," she explained. "All you have to do is move around and meet new people to realize how dumb you really are." For my mother the gilded volumes of *The Book of Knowledge* served as a self-help textbook on culture.

For me they were wondrous. I liked to lie on my stomach on the floor in front of the book case, my feet kicked up behind me, just taking in the strange and glorious pictures: Color illustrations in soft pastels from *The Book of the Dead*, which was left, the caption inaccurately tells us, "in the tombs of Egypt for the dead to read." A black-and-white cartoon of the globe in a ball cap, beaded in sweat and pulling down on a scale, to illustrate "Volume, Mass, and Weight." A four-page spread called "The Glory of the Grass" with detailed colored drawings of foxtail, rye, oat, timothy, manna, bearded darnel, broom, barley, reed, and wheat. Another four pages of "Beautiful Birds of the World" with a peacock in full array on the first page surrounded by a Blue Crowned Mot-mot, a Leadbeater's Cocatoo, and a Groove-Pigmy Goose along with nine other brightly-colored birds. And in volume eighteen, fourteen glorious pages of butterflies and moths and beetles by Rudolph Freund that begins with a Peacock Eye, an American species of butterfly, and ends 236 individual illuminated drawings later, with the European beetle called the Great Agrilus.

The famous frontispiece to the first edition of *The Children's Encyclopædia* shows a boy in knickers and girl in bloomers looking into an impossible universe of eight planets as well as comets, stars, and galaxies surrounding the sun which sends a halo of beams out into the darkness. But the inside cover illustration of each volume of *The Book of Knowledge* that I grew up with suggests a similar grandeur with a modern twist. A boy in shorts and a girl wearing a skirt stand alert and excited on a red book floating toward an island of worldly wonders including a telescope, a pagoda, totem poles, a factory, the faces of Mount Rushmore, and a giraffe. Overhead soar a rocket, a dual prop commercial airliner, a helicopter, and some sort of futuristic v-shaped space craft. "Here is a gift to the nation," Arthur Mee wrote to the readers of *The Book of Knowledge*. "It is a story that will never fail for children who will never tire; and it is the best of all stories, told in the simplest words, to the greatest of all ends."

~ ~ ~

And what is the end? On April 6, 1961, when I was eleven, my mother drove into a park near Deerfield, Illinois, where we lived at the time and killed herself with a gun. Whatever knowledge she had gleaned from those books, as well as all that was left in her heart and mind of love, joy, sorrow, and agony was swept away, too. The obliteration ripples out from there. My father did not talk about the past and the subject of my mother rarely came up after my father remarried and the family began anew. I remembered almost nothing of my life with her before the suicide except a few vivid flashes—images, really— the rest blown away by her death, and for years I was resigned to my ignorance and, perhaps, even content with it. I grew up, raised by a caring stepmother who probably got more than she bargained for when she took on my brother and me along with my dad, and I acquired a wonderful older stepsister. We did not dwell on our history. I went to college and married, and when I was in my thirties, my grandmother gave me the letters of my mother, but by then I had a job as a college professor and a family with four children. I worked hard and was not depressed or suicidal. Why would I want to read the letters of a mother who killed herself before I could even get to know her?

Recently, during a time of growth at the college where I teach, I was given a new office, and I used that change as an opportunity to discard files, magazines, and correspondence, the stuff that I had accumulated over the years. I threw away books that I thought I would never part with. My wife, Barbara, gave me a rule of thumb: if you feel the urge to sneeze when you open it, toss it out. In the end I threw away or recycled fourteen large plastic bags of junk, and drove back from the transfer station feeling lighter. But when I got to the boxes of my mother's letters, I could not throw them away. I held them in my hand—they were dusty and definitely gave me the urge to sneeze—but I could not shove them into a plastic trash bag.

I made a vow that if I kept them I would read them.

So, at the age of sixty-one, I bought a set of the 1952 edition of *The Book of Knowledge* like the ones I had read as a child and finally read my mother's letters through. There were 406 in all, carefully arranged by my grandmother in shoe boxes. Over time, as the family had leafed through them, they had gotten out of order and had been placed in different areas of the house before most were carted off to my office. It was not until six months after I finally brought them home that I spread them out on a pool table and put them in order. I boxed them and marked off each of the years with strips of manila cardboard, tickets to the past extending backward in time from 1960 to 1945.

My mother's writing style is direct and friendly, and—since she saw my grandmother as a confidante, especially in the early years of her marriage—often candid. As she got older, and more troubled, she tried to hide her depression, but she had become so used to confiding in her mother that the truth comes out anyway. She began the first letter on Saturday, September 29, 1945 with this declaration: "Today has been a big day" as she described going to college. She ends her last letter on May 31, 1960 about my brother and his classmates in a May Day program with the same undying hopefulness and sense of expectation: "they all did so well." In between, the letters tell the story of her Manichean struggle in the midst of the encroaching darkness of suicidal depression to maintain that openness to life's wonders, a battle that she eventually lost.

~ ~ ~

Barbara raised an eyebrow when I first mentioned my interest in the twenty volume set of *The Book of Knowledge* bound in ten thick books since she had been trying for several years to weed through the bookshelves at home just as I had at the office.

"Are you going to *buy* them?" she asked. I think she was making soup or maybe spaghetti.

"They have a set for $350 at Amazon."

Barbara, poker-faced, just kept stirring the pot.

Eventually I found a complete set available at AbeBooks on-line for $150, and put in my order. Sheepishly, I promised Barbara that I would keep the box they came in and resell them on-line as soon as I had finished with them.

When they arrived they were as magnificent as I had remembered, each handsome volume feeling heavy in the hand. Substantial, I thought, cracking open the cover of volume one. Quotations by the likes of Louis Bromfield, Eleanor Roosevelt, Captain Harry F. Guggenheim, the aviation pioneer, and Lou Little, the head football coach at Columbia University added authority to weight.

"The poet Marlowe might have been thinking of *The Book of Knowledge* when he spoke of 'infinite riches in a little room,'" Mrs. James P. McGranery, a member of the National Executive Committee of the Girl Scouts of the U.S.A. explained.

"There is only one good. That is knowledge," John S. Knight, the publisher of Knight Newspapers, announced, quoting Socrates while glowering under heavy brows at me from his photograph. He added a stern admonition.

"There is only one evil. That is ignorance."

We fanned the books out on the floor and began leafing through them, stopping at the colored spreads, Barbara running her fingers over the illuminated pages. The books spoke of a time after the Second World War when knowledge and progress and hope were allies, a time that she and I remembered dimly now as we ended the cynical first decade of the twenty-first century. Barbara found a page which asked, "Could We Ever

Travel to the Moon?" and I cringed at the outdated question, but she smiled. "Listen to this," she said later, reading at random an article in volume thirteen called "Government and Taxes" which argues that simply taxing in proportion to income, as the Constitution says, is unfair. "Taxes should be levied in such a way as to establish equality of sacrifice between rich and poor."

"Equality of sacrifice," she repeated. "Imagine that."

Before long she was eyeing the bookshelves we had been hoping to clear. "We'll make space right there."

"These books are pretty out of date," I said apologetically, opening a volume and resisting the urge to sneeze.

She was thinking about our new grandchildren.

"They could stand to read this."

She rapped the book with her knuckle. Decision made.

~ ~ ~

Wonder Question: Who holds the stars up?

The stars only appear to be nailed into fixed positions in the dome of the night sky and no one really holds them up for us. According to *The Book of Knowledge*, "all the stars—in fact, everything in the universe, asteroids, stars, galaxies of stars—all are moving through space at unbelievable speeds of many miles a second." The "great force of gravitation" holds them in check. "Each bit of matter in the universe pulls upon every other particle of matter. If one body comes too close to another body, the lesser is drawn into the greater and destroyed." But when the velocity of the objects and the distance between them is right they move in a controlled pattern. In the end this apparently accidental dance of forces is "responsible for the balance and state of equilibrium in the universe."

~ ~ ~

There was something more to my decision to read the letters than just changing offices. My life had been generally uneventful and happy, yes, but the ordinary losses were beginning to pile up and they didn't feel accidental. My kids had grown into adults and moved away, leaving a large house that I began to fill with projects. I began voluntarily stepping away from administrative duties at my college in the north Georgia mountains, my move to the office in the corner of my building a part of that shift. I felt no sadness in this change, embracing the notion that I would set aside these challenges, and, as I told everyone who asked, "just teach again," but I don't think that was really true. The gesture, the decision to step away from a busier life, was not a letting go, but a choice to clear a space for a more important task.

I remember one morning in particular standing at the edge of Butternut Creek, which runs through the woods at the bottom of the hill behind my house. The creek begins as a spring a few miles up the mountain from where I live and is fed by more springs along the way until it reaches my yard where it joins a separate tributary, nearly doubling in size. I glanced behind me, at the tumbling water, but soon turned, as I always do when I stand on this spot, to look toward the source of the stream. That is where I head when I leave the house and walk down the wooded path, not the tree-lined stream racing into the future, but the opening darkened by laurel at its source where rhododendron twist out of the ground like elongated arms and bayberry blossoms drip against a mossy bank. On this day I found myself gazing as usual into a thicket of privet beyond the foundered trunk of a fallen hickory toward the spring that is the origin of our mountain stream with my mother's letters still unread in their boxes on the pool table in my house, and knew that it was time to read them and follow their story back.

~ ~ ~

I had not forgotten everything about my childhood. I could remember well my father teaching me to shoot marbles with my thumb, throw a pocket knife, ride a bike, and do the long stretch while playing first base. I was able to recall hours alone, walking home from choir practice or school or gathering fossils in the back yard of our house in Nanuet. All of it came back vividly. If I closed my eyes, I could see the fossilized image of a trilobite cast in stone as clearly as when I held it in my hand more than fifty-five years before in our back yard in Nanuet, New York. What I could not see no matter how hard I tried were childhood moments with my mother. When I thought back on those places in my memory where I know she should be—the sofa, the TV room, the deck behind our house—she simply was not there. Even when I closed my eyes and tried to picture the scene I could not see her hands or face or eyes. I could not, and this is the heartbreaker, hear her voice. All of this—what do I call it?—this *mothering* was gone, wiped out by her death.

Who knows the psychology here? Part of it may be that the continuous mnemonic string snaps when a parent dies young. I can follow the thread of my father back along the lines of a life that managed to stretch well into my adulthood, the half-smile, cocked head, and jaunty manner I knew so well until he died refreshing with each visit the earlier versions of himself. But the string of experiences with my mother lies broken and frayed too far back in my life to sustain this continual remembrance. There is more, I'm sure. It was not just her absence, but the suddenness of her disappearance, and, no doubt, the violence and horror of it that was kept from me but implied in the silence surrounding the subject, that made the loss so thoroughgoing and complete. Her suicide exploded in my life like the flash of a camera at close range, darkening everything around me and casting me into blindness, and when the light returned she was gone. She did not fade, or slowly walk away, or whisper goodbye. She was there and she was not, and there was no getting her back. Ever.

That is probably enough to explain the lost memories, and I would like to stop here with this simple blast, but I know it is not the whole truth, because there is one more fold in the warm, and ultimately protective, blanket of my forgotten past. The months leading up to her death—months when she stopped writing letters at all and clearly gave up and spent most of her time alone with my brother and me—must have been so searingly sad and agonizing that I had buried them for good. These are the memories that come, if at all, in glimpses, like photos pinned on black velvet, and seem disconnected and bounded on all sides by an obscurity I cannot penetrate. The rest is darkness. I do not think she was mean, and I know that she never raised a hand to us in anger in her whole life, because the time that I did get a whipping from my stepmother, I felt the surprising sting of that for the first time. If I had to guess—and it is only a guess since there are no letters from this period—she was inconsolable, and I with my "bright" and "beaming" face full of curiosity and eagerness that she wrote about in many letters, and my brother who was the family clown, paraded our entire, pathetic routine in front of her slack expression and could not cheer her up. I had clues, those brief flashes of memory in which her face is hidden, when she stands with her back to me, a drink in hand, swaying to some sad song, or, late at night, after a shouting match with my father when I can catch a glimpse of her bent head from the top of the stair. I have carried those few, awful stills in my mind as my memory of her last year, and they glimmer, like apparitions at the gate of oblivion, saying do not, dear boy, enter this place of gloom.

And then, when I was old enough to absorb the blows, I sat down with the letters, boxes of them, and attending to her voice over the course of several weeks, my memories, lying like ashes in me, were sparked. When I read a sentence and absorbed a long forgotten detail in her words on the page, a small flame of remembrance occasionally ignited in some darkened chamber of my mind and a rocky seam opened in the glow and a hand appeared lifting an object or stepping out in front of it, or words, yes, spoken words, sounded once again in my thoughts, and as one sentence crawled across the paper and led to the next, and the next, the accumulated details shaped by her hand formed wholes in my mind and stories emerged, not narratives formed out of the sentences on the page, but the lost events themselves lumbering out of hibernation in that newly illuminated, subterranean hollow of mind where they had lain curled and dormant for decades, and my life, actual moments of it that I spent as a child with my mother, moments buried in the snowy winters of adulthood, rose upright at last into full consciousness.

The letters unburied our past together.

~ ~ ~

There was another gift, one that I probably was not prepared for until now, which explains, in part, why I have waited so long to open these envelopes and unfold the pages. The steady chronology of a letter or two each week allowed me to place the few vivid memories I had retained in a context so that I saw how they fit, and the stills, spliced into the larger film of my childhood, gave me enough of her story to understand why those last disconnected flashes from the awful and otherwise silent months at the end of her life had, of all in my lost past, remained as a glowing remnant.

Like an explorer, who comes across a trunk of maps, I set out on a journey into "terra incognita," along a trail of startling but familiar particulars, until I came upon a land that for all of its strangeness felt like home, an exotic Never, Never Land that had been waiting for me all the time. There I was, captured in words eternally as a boy, some Peter Pan who had refused to grow up, wondering where I had been all this time, a boy with a beaming face, the keeper of *The Book of Knowledge*, sitting Indian style in his pajamas in front of the bookshelves on the floor of the living room reading his way into the future. My father was there too, not the Captain Hook that I might want to make him out to be, but the actual man, ambitious, big-hearted, and flawed, the man whom I come to resemble more each passing day.

Most of all, I discovered at last my mother, not the stereotypical fifties mom forced to play an uncomfortable role, though she was that, but the real person with her achievements and flaws and hopes and many, many fears. As she left home for college, married, set up house with her new husband, and had children of her own, I watched her grow, darken, and retreat. The return addresses evolved from "Bobbie Reinhardt," a young nursing student in 1942 at the University of Kansas Hospital in Kansas City to "Mrs. M. J. Harvey" in Dodge City in 1947. By the time the family had moved to New York, she dropped the "Mrs." altogether, and in Chicago in 1959 retreated entirely by writing the return address using my father's name and title: "Dr. M. J. Harvey."

Every letter stood alone, capturing a particular time and mood, and yet each danced in consort with the others. As my mother married and had children, the mobile of her life grew heavier and more complicated, with many moving parts, and by the time of her death the structure groaned under the weight of accumulated anxieties and regrets, but reading allowed me to see, in the bobbing mixture of joy and damnation that these pages contained, our lives as a whole and to claim with her help a legacy of beauty and wonder from devastation.

I keep my mother's other memorabilia—all but her letters, that is—in a large, rectangular wicker basket in the storage room of my house. For a long time, this box of stuff was all I used to try to understand my mother's life and death. Occasionally when I was younger I would poke around in its braided plaits for mementos: a Glen Elder Citizenship award medal on a red, white, and blue ribbon kept in a silver Josten's box, a yellow newspaper celebrating the one hundredth anniversary of Glen Elder, four years' worth of high school report cards neatly signed by my grandmother. In addition to being an "A" student, my mother was absent only once in her entire high school career, an achievement honored with bound citations for perfect attendance that included "biographical sketches of our national presidents" on the back of each. There were several studio photographs, including one of her in profile, about age five, looking strikingly like my grandmother, and one of me at five or six wearing a suit with a vest and tie and a carnation pinned to my lapel. I am sitting amid a hundred or so young women in formal gowns from the night in 1955 when I was, for some reason, the "Crown Bearer of the Rainbow Girls" in Pearl River, New York. At the bottom of the basket, I once found a strip of white lace, snagged in the wicker as if by chance. When I tugged the end, it lifted free of the withes, followed by an ominous black ribbon.

Mostly this basket is filled with snapshots, lots of them, curled and yellowing and out of order, pictures of her and her family, mute testaments to the life I had lost. Pictures of my grandparents fishing on the Solomon River in Kansas or picnicking with family and friends, and pictures of my mother in Glen Elder, Kansas as a baby being bathed in a metal washtub, standing beside a toy tricycle in the shape of an airplane, and posing upside down in a silky costume doing acrobatics in the backyard. In her high school photo she looks demure in a crewneck cable sweater and her hands in her lap, her face slightly over-exposed. I have pictures of her riding horses with my dad when they first got married and lived in Dodge City where I was born. Pictures after my brother came along when we lived in Nanuet, including photos of us under her arms on a couch, and several of the whole family playing badminton with my mother looking sporty in clam diggers with a wide belt, a sleeveless top, and a bandana. Pictures from when we lived in Deerfield, Illinois, taking in the sights of Chicago with my grandparents, my grandfather looking fine having recovered remarkably from a stroke. I have the last picture of my mother alive standing beside me in front of our house on a sunny October day in 1959 when she looked happy but I suspect she was very ill, and pictures of her funeral and the funeral of my grandfather which happened within three weeks of each other.

The pictures always made me feel lonelier somehow. After I started my own family, I found myself turning to them now and then, enticed by the illusion of intimacy they offered. I would lift one out of the basket and marvel at the details that the camera caught, details I could never remember: my mother's long thin calves, the elegant tapering of her wrists, and her high forehead when she pulled back her hair with bobby pins. The fact that she wore bobby pins. Her cheeks appeared so smooth that I at times succumbed to the silly urge to touch them, only to be surprised by the hard, glossy surface. The photos promised spontaneity such as a curl out of place or the scuff marks on her two-toned saddle shoes, but it was precisely on this point—the matter of impulse—that the pictures ultimately disappointed me each time I pulled them out. The curl was eternally out of place, the smile remained tacked on forever, and the hand at the end of that elegant wrist hung midair like a stiffened claw. The images, I realized, are lifeless *mementos mori*, tattered and creased souvenirs of our loss, filled with little more than the emotions that we bring to them and drained of the life of their subjects.

"In the past when you looked at pictures of your mother's photographs you always saw a shadow in them," Barbara explained to me one morning while we were drinking coffee. It is true. There was nothing in most of them that gave a clue to her suicide, so I read her story not in the subject of the photo, but in the shadows draped in the background, which is not really her story at all, but my story of her. Even when she was not afraid, I saw fear. Even when she was not trembling, I supplied her trembling. Even when she was not consumed by thoughts of death, I shrouded her. Until I read the letters, those trembling shadows were where my search began and ended.

~ ~ ~

Wonder Question: "Does the earth make a sound as it rotates?"

17

"No," *The Book of Knowledge* that I am reading in my office at home answers, the "earth spins silently in space. It spins all in one piece, and that means not only the solid earth and the waters but the blanket of air above us as well. All spins round, never pausing." Like some enormous Carney ride, the globe rotates at a thousand miles per hour, and yet the mobile that Barbara gave me for Christmas hangs motionless in the corner by a thread, expectant and watchful as an acrobat holding a pose. "If the air stood still we might hear the earth whooshing through it," *The Book* explains, but the "air is part of the earth and moves with it" creating the illusion of stillness. Even if we could step off of the earth and stand on some promontory separate from the planet and listen hard, we would not hear the earth spinning. The scene would unfold like a slow-motion silent film, the incredible rush of the whirling planet registering on our eyes like the imperceptible motion of the slow hand on a watch and on our ears as a held breath. The other celestial objects would lumber along in mute procession with vast stretches of nothing at all between them. To hear any sound, "we must have vibrations, or waves, or trembling."

In space there is "no substance to be set trembling."

~   ~   ~

In one Brownie photograph from the wicker basket, my mother stands beside a tricycle with the shingled side of the house as the background. The front of the trike had a propeller with a circle of pistons behind it and the tailpiece at the end had numbers stamped in it to make it look authentic. The cockpit swooped down so that the rider could sit down completely and pedal. The toy is longer than she is tall, and it is clearly made of metal with dimples where bolts attach the wheels to the body. The wheels are inflatable rubber tires with shiny metal hubcaps. My mother poses proudly wearing Mary Janes, stockings, a pleated dress, a v-neck sweater, a beaded necklace, and a knit cap. She is dressed for cold weather and, since she was born in June, this is probably not a birthday gift but a Christmas present. And there is a shadow, perhaps the shadow of a tree, rising like a thin stream of smoke from behind her shoulder and spreading across the shingles of the wall, the adumbration, like the contrail of a plane in trouble, folding ominously and turning on her. Hurtling through space at a thousand miles an hour, my mother may be trembling a bit from the cold, but otherwise she does not feel the future rushing toward her. She cannot see the crash ahead. The air, after all, is moving too, at one with a planet of rocks and stones and trees, and spinning silently in a universe largely without substance. The girl who is my mother leans casually with her open hand on the wing of the toy while a ribbon of black billows across the shingles behind her smiling face.

She looks directly at me.

~ ~ ~

Wonder Question: Why do faces in some pictures seem to follow us?

"The rule is very simple," *The Book of Knowledge* says. "If the sitter is looking at the painter or at the camera, then wherever you stand, he will seem to be looking at you." I lift the photo of my mother beside her new toy and tilt it under the lamp, first to the right and then the left, and her eyes stay on me even though the nose of the airplane seems to bob away and return, the world of the photo turning on the axis of her eyes. And her smile— yes, it also seems to keep smiling at me, no matter which way I turn the stiff and fading image. But this rule, as stated here, is not so simple as *The Book of Knowledge* likes our wonders to be. There is the word "seem" in the phrase "he will seem to be looking at you" which is never simple. It drains the ink out of the words around it, appropriating them subjunctively. Nothing is looking at me in this photograph, although it is smiling broadly into the camera and trembling slightly in the cold, a trembling I can't feel because of the nothing she is and the nothing between us, and this nothing follows me no matter which way I turn.

~   ~   ~

I hold up another photograph of my mother and me taken in December 1952, the year my parents bought *The Book of Knowledge* and a month after my brother was born. Sitting together in the living room of our house in Nanuet, she and I are both dressed up. I'm not sure what the occasion might be, but she often took me shopping with her. Her dress also has a modern design made of small boxy squares in the fabric and the collar is cut away exposing a rectangle of skin at her neck. She does not wear a necklace, which this dress clearly calls for, but has bright, clip-on earrings, and sits upright holding me in her arms with her dark hair brushed back from her face. There are other boxes, too. The pole of a floor lamp glows behind her shoulder, and the sections of the shade and framed photographs beside it on the wall are all rectangles, completing the picture. And, of course, the picture is a rectangle, poorly cropped. If my father took it, he aimed too high, since I am only visible from the mouth up, my face and blond hair in an elaborate wave nearly white from the popping flash. My mother looks off and away, unaware that I am slipping out of the frame, and only my eyes, looking directly into the camera, hold me on the page, it seems, like two dark pins.

My mother looks pretty but in a severe way, with her arched eyebrows and dark lipstick. She is smiling, and her face, at twenty-six, is still young, though hard looking somehow, the cheek like a satin pillow, sleek on the surface but soft and vulnerable underneath. The photo is supposed to record a happy occasion, but like her letters it contains hints of anxiety: eyes dark at the corners, mouth tight, and a shadow at her chin that suggests quivering, as if the smile, held firmly in place, is about to crack as soon as the picture is done.

I am looking straight at the camera, and, as *The Book of Knowledge* says, my young face forever follows me now, no matter which way I tilt the photograph, the eyes unaware that I am looking back but curious and alert to the possibility that someone is watching on the other side of the camera. If the subject looks at the camera, the eyes will follow the viewer—that is the rule, but it has a tragic corollary: if the faces are not looking at the camera, "you can never get them to look at you," no matter which way you tilt the page. My mother is looking away in this photograph, her glance sidelong. Was she caught off guard? Did something on the TV catch her eye? Did my baby brother move or cry or distract her? Did she have a sudden regret and look off? Who knows? No matter how many ways I tilt the page, my mother in this photo looks away from me forever.

~ ~ ~

Even when a picture breaks the rule about the eyes, it still hides its secrets. I take another photograph out of the wicker basket. My father, mother, brother and I are on a sofa looking at the camera. My mother has on a sheer summer dress with cap sleeves. Hair up, she wears earrings, and her expression is hard to describe. Serene is not the right word, though her skin is smooth, the

21

muscles of the face relaxed, and her eyes are free of shadows or lines. The mouth wants to smile, makes the faint gesture at the corners to lift, but if it is a smile it is half-hearted, nothing like the broad grins that my father and I wear. It is the eyes though that startle. Framed, as always, by the nearly perfect half-circles of her eyebrows and enclosed in the oval of her lashes, the pupils themselves are unfocused. They are not tired or listless, exactly, but empty, as if some part of her is gone. The picture breaks the rule. She looks directly into the camera, and I tilt the photo back and forth to catch her eye, but no matter which way I turn it, her eyes refuse to follow me.

~ ~ ~

Before I read the letters I picked up bits of my mother's story indirectly, often in fits and starts, and pieced together some of what had happened in the last year of her life on my own. In addition to the photos, I had several handwritten versions of my grandmother's autobiography on seven sheets of typing paper, and these notes, which arrived with the wicker basket, filled in gaps. In November 1960 she "got word" that my mother was in the hospital. The passive voice is portentous. It means that my mother was in no condition to write or phone and that my father, whom my grandmother never trusted, had to break the news. I close my eyes and try to imagine the call. I can hear the tone of the conversation, my dad offering up the facts through the mixture of sympathy and complaint he used to calm anxious colleagues, and my grandmother, with her Kansas reticence, replying in tight-lipped, staccato phrases. But I cannot even begin to imagine their words. My grandparents "left immediately by train for Deerfield" where they stayed with my brother and me until my mother killed herself five months later.

My grandmother never talked to me about what happened when my mother was institutionalized for depression during this time, but she did talk to Barbara, who wrote letters to her on a regular basis until my grandmother died in 1986, and was probably my grandmother's dearest confidante at the end of her life. She told Barbara that when they released my mother from the hospital, the doctors said that they "had done everything that they could" and were still pessimistic. "When she left the hospital your grandmother knew she would do it," Barbara said when I asked her about it recently. She had told me about the conversation before but to make her point clear now she put it this way: "when she left *that morning*," on the day she killed herself, "your grandmother *knew* she would do it."

After I graduated from college, I asked my father about my mother's death. We were riding in silence in his car early in the morning. It was still dark outside, the only light the blue glow from his dashboard. I know he didn't want to talk about her, but he wanted to answer my questions. Nothing made her happy, he told me, and the doctors could do nothing for her. "They tried everything," he said, an echo of my grandmother's words. He said that she bought a .44 caliber gun which is a large bore. "She *meant* to do it—to end things." So she drove to the lake and killed herself. He may have said "park," not "lake," but I heard "lake." It pained him to say these words, I could tell. I do not want to underestimate the difficulty of living with someone who is clinically depressed. I know, now, from reading her letters that he tried to make her happy, and he was very good at making others feel happy, but in the long run he could not work that charm on her. He took a long drag from his cigarette, squinted, and stuffed the butt in his ashtray slowly exhaling the smoke as the car hurtled down the highway, waiting for my next question. We rode silently into a predawn darkness illuminated by the blue light from the dash.

The rest was left to my imagination.

~ ~ ~

One measure of my confusion is an essay called "Suicide Notes," published in my first book in 1993, in which I imagined the scene of her suicide. Here is what I wrote:

> She stops to tug at a loose lock of hair (the one that always falls on her forehead) and scoots in front of the rear-view mirror to fix it. A glimpse of the end of time, an appropriation of the future in an instant—that's suicide. Like a wedding photo it's posed, intended for a dignified spot on the mantel.
>
> She can't be thinking of the truth—of the way she will look after the shot, the gore that makes some poor bather step back. She can't be thinking... no, it is the framed view in the car mirror she sees as she purses her lips and tucks back loose hair—a final pose she intends to pass down, a pose but for the holding held forever, and in deference to the intention, I see it. I do. I see it for as long as I can—I do.
>
> But she takes a breath and the pose, as poses do, gives away more than intended. It is a pretty snapshot creased by worried hands, and I who keep the picture for a lifetime must face the other truth: the gobs of flesh splattering the back of a driver's seat, two quick and ugly involuntary jerks, blood pumping and sucking a gash, a lock of hair that tumbles out of place no

24

matter what she does, and the idiot eyes rolled back, and back some more.

Of course, I got it all wrong. *All* wrong. *The framed view in the car mirror?* You can tell I had been looking at too many pictures. She was not even in the car. She stepped out of it to kill herself. She was in a park, not by the lake. There was no bather, but a patrolman who saw what happened. I have no idea what she was thinking or what impression she intended to leave behind. She was depressed so I doubt that she cared about her appearance or looked in the mirror at all, and the comparison to the wedding photo is bullshit.

Complete bullshit.

I no longer trust my imagination of that day.

~ ~ ~

By itself, *The Book of Knowledge* is also little help. After it arrived, I spent a morning searching the index for clues, and when I was done, sat back disappointed. In its 7,606 pages, *The Book* has no entry for suicide. It has no entry for insomnia, alcoholism, or addiction either. There is an entry for ragweed, but not for rage. In the age of anxiety there is no entry for anxiety, and no entry for depression without Great in front of it. The entry on sex is limited to plants and flowers. There is no entry for conformity or blandness or dullness or insipidity, and this is the 1950s! Sometimes I wonder about *The Book of Knowledge.* Clearly I need to darken its cheerful entries. I find an entry for Peter Pan, of course, but none for Cyril Richard. No entry for either "Fever" *or* Peggy Lee. Nothing on the doldrums, the dumps, the mulligrubs, or the blues. No blue funk or the blahs. Nothing on grief—*grief!* No entry for funeral, burial, interment, last rites, cortège, mourners, pall bearers, or pall. No entry for self-murder, self-slaughter, self-destruction, and no entry for self. No entry for hara-kiri (which is a little surprising) or suttee (which is not). There are several entries under medicine, but no cure for despair, despondency, sadness, sorrow, unhappiness, melancholy or gloom. I need to create some wonder questions of my own since doom does not make the pages of *The Book of Knowledge*. Nor agony nor suffering nor woe. In *The Book of Knowledge*, no *woe*!

~   ~   ~

Wonder Question: What is everything?

In the late 1950s, after the doctors try everything else, they strap my mother to a gurney in a hospital room and tape the leads of a heart monitor to her chest. They do not inject her with an anesthetic for pain or use muscle relaxers to reduce the chance of bone fractures and other injuries when the arms, legs, and breasts rise against the restraints, but they do place a block in her mouth so that she cannot bite her tongue while the procedure is performed. They attach electrodes on either side of her face at the temples after applying a conductive jelly so that an electrical current passes into her head and brain more easily. Once she is ready, the doctor turns on a machine which sends a steady stream of electricity into her skull, the current running between the right and left lobe of her brain for twenty seconds inducing a *grand mal* seizure and leaving her unconscious, probably for about a half-hour. No one knows for sure what happens in her brain as her eyes roll back and her body stiffens. The shock of electricity may slow overly agitated mental activity or dull brain receptors altering her mood. It may release neuropeptides that ease depression. Or it may cause brain damage. Electroshock therapy helps many people, but, as one critic put it, the procedure is "like playing Russian roulette with your brain."

Steven Harvey

What is everything in the late 1950s?
It is a very sad figure of speech come true.

~   ~   ~

I remember when I was eleven, that I often lay in bed at night listening to my parents fight downstairs. The arguments began as conversation mixed with the clinking sound of ice in glasses, the words spoken softly, clipped and brittle, dipping to near inaudibility when whispered like the clicking of tree branches that is prelude to the storm. Eventually the voices rose until the two were shouting and finally screaming furiously, the sound coming through the walls in unarticulated growls. I don't think they ever hit each other, but sometimes they broke glasses and ashtrays. Dad may have caught her arms when she took drunken, limp, and futile swings at him. I think I saw that once.

I was too afraid when they fought to move and lay wrapped under a cocoon of sheets and blankets that felt like safety but acted like an echo chamber amplifying and distorting the low rumble until the roar, punctuated now and then with a slam or a crash, spilled over me. I waited, understanding nothing, absorbing it all. It was only when the yelling was done that the silence after the curses brought me out of bed to the top of the stairs to be sure that they were all right. I usually walked down a few steps and leaned forward, peering between the balusters in order to see into the kitchen, blinking at the fluorescent glare. One night, the night I remember, they caught me. I can picture the tableau even now. My dad, his sleeves rolled up facing a wall, my mother sitting bent over in a kitchen chair with her back to him, crying in gasps.

"Oh no," she says when she turns, mascara running down her cheek, and sees me running back upstairs.

27

I see in memory the mascara, but not the face. How can that be?

The next day my father pulled me aside and asked what I had heard.

"You were fighting," I said.

He corrected me. They were not having a fight, but a "discussion."

"That's what adults do," he said.

The fight followed by the conversation with my dad is one of my few vivid memories of my mother. It glows with borrowed light like an object near a lit match in the darkness that is my past, a little flame that I followed into the dark until it flickered out. Here is another lit match. From my bedroom I see a light in the hall, soft this time like the glow of a candle. Drawing the twisted sheets up around my shoulders, I hear the clank of the changer and the long wavering whoosh and whir when the needle hits the disc. Clink of ice in a glass. Swoosh of a magazine dropped to the floor. My mother turns up the volume, and soon Peggy Lee's voice fills the house to the corners, beating back gathered silence. I slip out of bed and hide at the top of the stairs to watch. Snapping fingers, slapped cymbal, thud of a double bass and drum, and a lone, plaintive female voice. Mom's there alone, her back to me, her profile partially visible, lit by the glow of the console. She sways, drink in hand, and sings, watching the record spin, holding the notes out for no one, trying to sound good.

"What a lovely way to burn," she croons. "What a lovely way to burn."

~ ~ ~

So even without the letters I can—from family stories, the memorabilia, the photographs, and some research—line up a few of the events of my past and trace the outline of what happened. The fights and my mother singing "Fever" occurred in 1960 before my grandparents moved in with us in November. Peggy Lee's new song, "Fever," was the rage, and my parents had the album in their record collection, and this record followed my family long after my mother died. I remember it because of the distinctive cover photograph of Peggy Lee in a black cocktail dress, her pale skin and platinum blonde hair set against a blue background. The album was released in May 1960. So the fights and the drinking alone while singing into the stereo console must have happened between May and November of 1960, in the time just before my grandparents arrived and Mother was hospitalized for depression.

At this point the letters supply a few dates that help make the story-line clear, but it was a story that all of us had figured out before I read them. During 1959 and 1960 my dad was gone most of the time on business trips and to take courses in business management in St. Louis. "Max has been in St. Louis," my mother writes on March 26, 1959, and on July 9 she mentions that "Max has been to St. Louis since Tues. will be back tomorrow." These business trips to St. Louis run like a refrain after 1959 until the letters come to an abrupt halt in June 1960, within a month of the release of the album that contains "Fever." The memory of that song may be the last message I have from my mother since it came after the last letter.

My stepmother tells me that she met my father in St. Louis around this time, but my mother seems unaware of infidelity during 1959 and early 1960. In the letters she appears to be genuinely concerned about the problems related to his job. What upset her was the pressure that the management position put on their lives, and she urged him to quit. It had done damage to their friends, some of whom became alcoholics, made my father ill, and saddled my mother with social responsibilities she could not handle. It is clear, in retrospect, that she was clinging to a symptom of the problem, and had no handle on the real problem in their relationship. I sense in all of the letters from my mother at that time her desire to live in a way that reduced the strain on everyone, and I suspect that the conversation about leaving the company was real on her part, but doomed on his, because his job at Cyanamid was not what divided them.

My father's energy, the competitive urge to succeed that drove him to work long hours and travel for months at a time, was a part of his personality, a rapaciousness for life that my mother who retreated from power, and too often joy, didn't share. Dad's ulcer and her exhaustion may have reinforced the idea that their loveless marriage had to do with the demands of his career, not another woman, but it was the force of will that he brought to all he did that really divided them, whether it was playing quarterback for Whittier College or going for a business degree or wooing clients in a duck blind in Maryland.

A deep-seated loneliness beyond his job drove my father out of our house week after week and eventually required solace, the arms of a woman willing to join him without holding back. Sometime in June of 1960 my mother must have put the clues together. When she did, the letters stopped.

"Captain Smith loved Pocahontas," Peggy Lee sings in a verse that she wrote and added to her version of the song. They "had a very mad affair."

The depression that perched on my mother's life and led to her suicide on April 6, 1961, had many parts, but here is one black wing: On April 29, three weeks and two days after my mother's death, Dad married my stepmother.

"What a lovely way to burn," Peggy Lee growls four times at the end of "Fever." "What a lovely way to burn."

In the penultimate line Lee's voice rises in desire on the first word—"What"— before it slides down the "lovely way" to the last note, "burn," dying like the flicker of a heartache.

And the final line?

It is a scorched whisper, a beckoning, and a come on. It is a raised eyebrow. "What a lovely way to burn."

~ ~ ~

Wonder Question: What secrets do the stars contain?

"In early times," *The Book of Knowledge* says, "astronomers believed that many different kinds of events could be foretold by the positions of the stars and planets." Ancients used the predictable movements of heavenly objects to determine when to plant and harvest, so it "was only natural" for them to believe that stars had an influence over other human affairs. Birthdays are clues to the kind of person the newborn will be and Zodiacal signs offer ambiguous indicators about life ahead. It was "a common belief that all kinds of human events could be predicted by observing the heavenly bodies."

Is suicide a secret hidden in the stars? *The Book* is skeptical. "There are," it says with a sigh, "many people today who believe in astrology," but the resigned tone only irritates me. There *must* be "something substantial" between us and the stars, some sympathy.

After all, they seem to tremble like us from dusk until dawn.

~ ~ ~

My mother died on the day that my father planned to leave the family for good. He intended to start a new life for himself in Kentucky without my mother or my brother and me. Was he anxious or exhilarated when he left the house that April morning, relieved or scared? Or some other emotion I cannot even imagine. If on that day my grandmother knew what my mother would do, he may have too, but I'm not sure because, unlike my shrewd grandmother, he was an optimist. After he left, my mother bought the gun, drove to the park, stepped out of her car, and pulled the trigger. My grandparents, who knew it would happen, were taking care of my brother and me. When Dad found out, he came back for us.

The memory of his return is another of those few mental snapshots that I retained on the black velvet board in my mind. In it I am alone downstairs, killing time, when my dad arrives and the house begins to fill with neighbors and my parents' friends. I am spinning below them in our newly renovated den, holding a balsa wood *Jetfire* glider that I kept in a hiding place under the stairs. I usually got the planes at the five and dime when I visited my grandparents in Glen Elder, but they must have brought this one to me because the memory is in Illinois. I can still clearly picture these planes that I assembled myself and studied for hours. The wings are stamped with red designs marking the ailerons and flaps and labeled on one side with the name of the company, "Guillows," and on the other with the name of the plane, "Jetfire." The cockpit is embossed on the fuselage and inside a pilot with a red helmet leans forward. Meant to ride breezes, the glider is light in my hand. It has a small piece of metal folded over the nose for protection when it crash lands against the walls of the house or the concrete driveway, which is most of the time, but I am not allowed to fly it indoors, so I hold it and spin, making airplane noises and getting dizzy. When I stop the room seems to keep on spinning, and I wobble a bit as if I have taken a blow. I'm almost twelve. Too old to be doing this sort of thing.

I have been taken out of school, and I don't know why.

I hear the ringing doorbell of each new arrival upstairs. The hushed greetings. The whispers. The shuffle of feet over carpet as adults overhead approach each other. I am pretty sure that no one has told me what has happened yet. Dad would do that when we were on the train going to Kentucky. But I know *some*thing because I hide under the stairs in my favorite hideaway and sit there a long time before anyone notices my absence. This is where I keep the plane and a small, metal pirate's chest filled with fossils and a rabbit's foot. Overhead, the points of the nails that had been used to secure the treads to the risers of the stairway protrude. Like stars they glitter in the crawl space, and I look into them as I listen to the groan in the floorboards. Suddenly it grows silent, and I hear my father call for me. At first his voice is a question, but then, freighted with all of the tension of that day, it becomes a barked command. Soon others join in, their anxious voices a keening chorus of my name.

On the day of my mother's death, I stare into trembling stars nailed into the night sky of my own making without a clue.

"Who holds the stars up?" Marjorie Mee asked her perplexed mother.

A shadow passes over the risers.

I cover my ears.

~ ~ ~

Last September when Barbara and I visited my stepmother in Kentucky, we spent a Saturday morning looking through a box of pictures that she kept in her attic. In her eighties, she pulled them out of boxes one at a time with arthritic fingers, stopping occasionally to talk, and the subject came around to my mother.

"No honey," she said when I asked if my mother bought the gun before that day. I'm sitting across from her at the kitchen table. Barbara, who is standing, stops flipping through pictures and listens. "She bought it that morning. She killed herself in the park. A policeman saw her and thought it unusual for a woman to be in the park alone, so he followed her. She stepped out of the car and then."

My stepmother put her finger to her temple and lifted her eyebrows.

"Bam."

I look away. A cat waits in a crouch under the bird feeder in her neighbor's yard. I want to hate my stepmother for doing that, for being so distant from these events that she turns them into a cartoon. I have trouble getting the image out of my mind, her lips puckering on the single syllable, her finger on the trigger and her thumb tripping like an imaginary hammer. Barbara looks at her, and then me, dismayed I can tell, but also willing to let the moment pass without comment, urging me, with her glance, to do the same. She turns back to the pictures that she is flipping through. These events happened long ago involving a woman my stepmother never met. I may be hearing hard truths about my mother, but she is talking about a stranger, in plain language which is her way, and what she really wants to describe is her own loneliness and desperation.

"Neither of us had anybody," she said, referring to the time when she and my father first met in a bar, explaining that her first husband was impossible to live with, too. "I had nobody. Your dad had nobody."

Nobody.

Silenced for a moment by that story, we return to the pictures. Many of them show my stepmother with my dad through the years, but I pause over one in particular. In it, the two of them are preparing dinner. They both are young. My dad, heavy set in a dark shirt and white trousers, has turned, startled by the picture, and his face, picking up the full impact of the flash, wears a customary carefree and bold look. He's making a salad and is probably about to tell a joke. The flash explodes like a supernova on the sliding glass door behind him, turning the rest of the glass black.

It is the image of my stepmother that holds my attention, though. She stands in the wood-paneled room, looking young and very pretty in a striped sweater and tight slacks, her nose aquiline and her hair all dark curls. She leans toward my father from behind as if she has some secret to share, but the easy-going intimacy of the photograph keeps no secrets. He came to her in St. Louis for fun, happiness, love, and sex. He came to escape a house full of woe, some of it of his own making—some, but certainly not all. He was leaving us for this, that was the secret, and when my mother figured it out, she gave my brother and me to him, to them, with a single gunshot.

~ ~ ~

Wonder Question: "What is the sound of everything happening at once?"

"When a gun goes off," *The Book of Knowledge* says, "the flash and the report of the gun occur in the same moment." If we stand at a distance, the flash appears first, as a silent flare in the darkness, and the muffled blow of the sound arrives later, in an echo of the flash. So, if you stand at a safe distance half a mile away when the gun is fired, "you will not hear the sound for nearly half a minute."

"And yet," *The Book of Knowledge* adds, "if we are very near the gun, we see the flash and hear the noise at the same time." At that range, you miss nothing. If you hold the gun to your body, you feel everything happening at once, and it reverberates until the trembling stops somewhere at the edge of nothing.

~ ~ ~

Suicide. Turning the self into nothing. It is a moral conundrum too difficult for *The Book of Knowledge* to crack. A literal self-contradiction, the answer even eluded Jesus. The Catholic poet Dante may have planted the suicides with other violent sinners in a deep ring of hell, and tormented the poor souls with winged harpies, but the golden rule is about doing unto others, not doing the self in, and on suicide Jesus is silent. It wasn't until the nineteenth century that Immanuel Kant, whom some consider the wisest European philosopher, explained the immorality of suicide logically with his "categorical imperative." When faced with a moral dilemma, Kant argued, you should act so that your action becomes universal law. When you lift a gun to your temple to pull the trigger, you must imagine that the hands of all of the people in the world are required by your version of the moral law to lift a gun to their temples, too. No one escapes the bullet in this game of Russian roulette. Do you like this vision of the world, Kant asks?

I give it a try and see my mother in the hall of mirrors within her moral imagination, every hand in the world holding a .44 lifted at her command, and she pulls the...but, no, that is not right.

Suicide is about the survivors.

Suicide is two boys and a father hurtled into the darkness at the speed of a locomotive. The boys, sitting on the plush pile seat of a railroad car headed away from their home in Deerfield, Illinois, will never see their mother again, rarely speak of her again, rarely think about her again. Their father—a big man, bulging out of his suit—sits down on his haunches in front of them. Facing into the darkness ahead, he has been through hell and has been given one more impossible task, but he is a man who believes in taking charge and wants to fix things even when he can't, so he will do his job. Having lost their mother, the boys facing their father in the passenger car are headed backward into the night, the lights outside the window floating away from them, and I don't know if they are afraid or in shock or just tired.

Who knows what the younger one remembers of that night? He is eight years old and has penetrating blue eyes. In his memory, this happened in a car, not a train, but I remember it happening first on a train, my dad looking down but only for a moment and then, as he always did when he spoke to people, looking directly into our eyes. I remember him speaking, his voice a mesmerizing low rasp conveying confidentiality this time as well as command, and I remember him reaching out with his arms to kind of hem us in as he spoke, his large arms coming out of the sleeve of his suit a bit as he extended them. I remember—or I think I do—the maroon plush of the seats and the windows black as we rode into the open fields of Illinois at night.

But I have no idea what he said.

~ ~ ~

The saddest picture in my wicker basket shows my mother's open casket surrounded by a shower of flowers, a mound of red and white carnations, daisies, and pink mums. When I hold it to the light, I can see that the coffin is draped in a spray of red roses, and my mother's body lies in a bed of satin, the opening of the casket draped in a transparent mesh. The picture of her face is very small, but I can see that her hair is pulled back from her forehead in tight curls. She wears a suit with a silk scarf at the neck, exposing the base of her throat. I find a magnifying glass that I keep with my dictionary, and examine the picture up close. The cotton and plaster of Paris that the morticians used to reconstruct the face make her cheeks look puffy and the dermal wax and restorative cosmetics hide her wounds and bruises under a shiny pastiness betraying the illusion of life. There is something wrong with the mouth that has been stretched wide into a smile after the mortician pulled together the scalp, and the eyebrows are heartbreaking, dark and perfectly arched like wings, as if, after all, death took her by surprise, and maybe—who knows?—it did.

My gaze settles at last on her eyes, the seat of the soul. Leaning forward into the lens to see more clearly, I tilt the page this way and that for a better look, before slumping back into my chair.

Faces in photos don't follow us if their eyes are closed.

~ ~ ~

For most of my life, this story, ending with this photograph, was all I had, a shadowy sequence of events, pieced together, with little sense of what the person at the center of it all was like. I could see her in the pictures, but not in memory, and I could not hear her voice. That silence, was, I think, what my mother wanted. Eternal silence. She planned to disappear leaving behind the after-images of her life to fade in a wicker basket along with her old report cards and twists of lace. She wanted her face to wear a death mask that her sons, in particular, could not penetrate. She was buried in a windswept graveyard in Kansas, and I suspect that she would have liked the idea of a headstone facing off on an open prairie, her story unwritten and unwritable, a series of questions without answers. If my grandmother had not saved her words and passed them on to me she would have gotten her wish.

~   ~   ~

On the word "wish" I stop typing, close the book in my lap, and walk to the window that faces on my back yard. After three days of rain, the morning is sunny and the beans that I planted in a box garden hang heavy, all bumpy and knotted, on vines, some long and stringy, others curled into sickle shapes. A chipmunk with several stripes down its back, like the kind I used to see as a boy, darts out from the railroad ties that hold back the hill from the back door and, sensing my presence, freezes in the yard. Sunbeams slash through hardwood trunks, the beams filtered by the last of the morning fog clearing off the mountain. Beyond that slope into the woods the creek rushes from its source carrying its glitter away.

In the past when I tried to piece together the events surrounding my mother's death, I was thwarted by a lack of substance. I felt like a Titan arranging the planets, enormous objects so light and airy in their concentric orbits that merely tapping them caused them to float off. They lacked the ballast of story. Connected in the soup of their nearly weightless suspension, they were held in check by the invisible tug of gravity, but I didn't understand the secret of their interrelationships so each time I touched one, others slipped away like weightless objects in space. Tap the earth and it sets the stars twinkling as it slumps down in its billowing skirts of air and clouds. Tap the sun and the moon floats off in compensation, like a flipped Liberty dollar.

But after I read the letters and started writing I discovered that the pictures had a script. They were no longer just clues, but illustrations of a narrative that played out before me in panorama. Like the dead in the

Odyssey who stand as apparitions before the hero at the bloody fosse, these filmy images did not breathe, but at last they spoke, and I heard the voices as if for the first time telling me what I may have suspected but didn't know. I sensed an order in my past, the unfolding of a story that included a family in some netherworld described in a narrative drafted by my mother, guarded by my grandmother, and left for me to tell, but rather than feel emboldened at last to write our story down, I felt bereft. I had been protected from all of this, I realized, and some part of me acknowledged in the silence of this room my mother's unspoken admonition to stop and not go on. Allow the planets and stars of my life to line up, but don't ask why. *Heed* this silence, the room says, the quiet like a hand touching my sleeve in the face of characters lining up with blood on their lips, requesting permission to speak. *Honor* it as a last wish. I waited long enough for the chipmunk to gather his courage and dash for the wall before turning and walking back to my seat at the desk where the blinking cursor had been holding my place.

"Woody Herman's music is sweeping the nation," my mother wrote in one of her earliest letters. It was 1945 when Kansas City was a jazz hub. My parents—Max and Bobbie—were dating and caught up in the swirl: shopping, going to shows, dancing all night in clubs. Dad drove down U.S. 40 from Manhattan where he went to school to pick her up at the university, and they often bounced from town to town on the way into the city following the music and twisting to "the boogie." Sometimes they stopped at "roadside parks" for picnics where Dad cooked steaks over a wood fire. In one letter, dated October 7, my mother describes an all-nighter filled with excitement and music. It began with a trip to Topeka where Dad bought "a beautiful brown suit" and my mother purchased "a black slip and bra, good white scarf, and a black purse." She was ready for a night on the town: "At last I have my outfit."

They drove to Lawrence to pick up their friends Neal and Shirley at the bus station, and headed off for "KC," arriving about six. "We stopped at the Interlude," and "had steaks and listened to Joshua Johnson," who played piano boogie.

The main event though was Woody Herman. "He's Coming," the newspaper clipping that fell out of the envelope of mother's letter announced, "The Country's Greatest Dance Band." Herman would be in Kansas City "for one night" in his "only Midwest appearance." His orchestra included Francis Wayne as the vocalist and other "stars" of the Midwest jazz scene: Chubby Jackson, Flip Phillips, and Bill Harris.

My parents and their friends arrived at the Municipal auditorium about 8:30. "It is a huge building one block square," my mother wrote, agog. They worked their way through the crowd to the front of the room, "right below the stage," and were there when the musicians "took their places." In 1945, Woody Herman's star was on the rise. He and his orchestra, called "The Herd," had just signed a contract with Columbia, recording hits like "Laura" and "Caldonia." The next year Herman and his orchestra played Carnegie Hall and won awards from *Billboard*, *Metronome*, and *Esquire* as the top band in the country. My mother's reaction was mixed. The musicians "were peculiar looking" and Herman's style was too flashy for her taste. "Even on sweet and mellow pieces he always has to end it up with jump and jive." She preferred the more conventional sound of Les Brown, but admitted that the musicians in Herman's band "sure could play" and that the audience was "wild about it."

The room was too crowded for dancing. "We stood there jammed against the stage for two hours," my mother complained. "Finally Shirley & I could stand it no longer because our feet were killing us." The two of them went to the balcony and watched from there until 12:45 when the band stopped. By the time the concert was over, all of the restaurants in the city were "jammed with people" so they headed to Lawrence to drop off Neal and Shirley, eating in Ottawa, a town along the way, and talking until 4:30 in the morning. "We had to talk fast and furious to keep awake." Later they ate a breakfast in Wamego and reached Manhattan at eight o'clock where my dad dropped off my mother on his way to start work, without sleep, at nine.

~ ~ ~

When I read the letters, my mother sashayed back into my life, staying up late, wearing smart clothes, and falling in love. I picture her leaning over the pen as she wrote with the empty page of stationery under her fingertips thinking of the next word and looking off into the future, and the death mask that I had carried within me for years relaxes into a face. "What happened to the woman I married?" my father asked once, and it's a good question. The letters allowed me to ask what happened to that woman as well. My mother clearly was attracted to Dad's excitement. She liked a pretty outfit with a black purse and fancy undergarments, danced the boogie-woogie, stayed up all night to hear jazz, ate steak dinners, "had more fun"—as in the phrase "we had more *fun*"—at the show *Anchors Aweigh*, clowned around with the "pepsters" in her sorority, ate "raw eggs" for the heck of it, and asked my dad out to the "gold-digger's ball."

Yes, that woman. What happened to her?

~ ~ ~

I do not know when my parents met, but in the first letter my dad shows up taking her to a football game on September 29, 1945 and the relationship was already serious, with jazz as the backdrop. That evening there was going to be live music at a varsity dance, but Dad had to work. Always the fixer aiming to please, he loaned my mother a radio to listen to the Hit Parade, but she was still unhappy. "We don't get to go," she moped. "Sure wish I could." She loved to dance, and Dad introduced her to a world of music, parties, and carefree joy that she probably had not known, and they had already talked of marriage, though there were tensions just under the surface of the relationship from the beginning. At the close of the semester, she was accepted into the nursing program at the University of Kansas Hospital, and the conflicts between her and Dad began to emerge.

One night, sitting among friends at the college canteen, she broke some bad news to my dad. If she entered the program she would only have six weeks of vacation and the first vacation was only a week long. Dad grew sullen. "Six weeks, my God," he grumbled several times as she and their friends tried to change the subject. He had plans to set up a veterinary practice in Dodge City, his hometown in the western part of the state, and hoped that she would drop out of school and marry him. "Bobby," he blurted out angrily, "one week wouldn't give us *time* to get married."

Her parents had been applying pressure from the other side when marriage seemed likely, urging my mother to finish school. They had always been protective of their only daughter and suspicious of this smooth-talker who was as comfortable in boots as in a suit, liked jazz and cars and dancing and fat steaks, and didn't seem to have established himself yet. In the end, they were probably glad for any plans that might slow down a wedding. She was caught in the middle. "I do want to please you," she had written to them, feeling anxious about being left to dangle between these alternate visions of her life. "It is such a hard decision and not a single person can help me."

"Everything inside of me tells me this isn't the thing to do," Dad told her at the canteen after his anger had subsided. "There is only one thing in the world I want" he said, speaking directly to her at this table of friends, "and that is to be married to you—and if this is the only way it can be accomplished," he added, defensively, "there isn't much I can say."

~ ~ ~

Wonder Question: Why do two sides of a road seem to meet in the distance?

If you stand in the middle of a highway and look down its length, the *Book of Knowledge* explains, the road will appear to get narrower even though the sides of the road run in parallel lines. The place in the road where you are standing "may be forty feet or more in width," but if you look ahead down that long stretch, miles into the distance, "the width will grow less and less" and the opposing edges of the highway will appear to meet at a point on the horizon. "This is an effect of what artists call perspective" in which close objects loom large and distant ones appear to shrink in size.

~ ~ ~

My mother signed up for classes in pharmacology, surgical nursing, medical nursing, professional adjustment, nursing arts II, and diet therapy. "Sounds like we'll be busy, doesn't it," she wrote, warily. She quickly made friends with the twelve other students in the program: "it is practically like living in a sorority except the girls are a lot friendlier." The bonding became stronger as they studied late into the night for tests and did rounds on the cancer ward together. The patients, who were mainly older women and "pretty grouchy," were difficult. "They act like we're machines to do their any whim no matter how busy we are," she complained. The new nurses finished each shift exhausted: "Every one

45

of us new students flops on the bed the minute we get back to our rooms after we've been on duty."

She found that nursing was rewarding: "I'm so glad I came into training." She called it a "self-satisfying profession" and said that she "always looked forward to going on the floor." She surprised herself with the reservoir of kindness that she and the other nurses drew on to do their work. "It's amazing how sweet and patient you can be." Procedures, such as a "sitz bath" or the "ortho prep" done before surgery may have sounded daunting in class but they were actually simple in practice, and sometimes it was exciting to be part of such important work. "Guess what I just got through seeing?" she wrote after observing a delivery: "A Caesarian." Even the depressing duty of working with terminal patients did not get her down. "The patients on 4b (the floor we are on) are mostly late cancer patients. The prognosis of my patient is unfavorable. She has cancer of the uterus and they have given her two transfusions this week." Working amid so much hopelessness did not discourage her. "If this is the worst, I think I'll be very happy."

I imagine her returning to the dorm after a shift in the cancer ward, setting her shoes at the foot of her bed, and crawling under the covers too tired to take off her uniform. I'm sure that she missed her fiancé who was a day's drive away, but I get no sense that she was lonely, and in my mind she is smiling as she turns her head on the pillow and falls asleep. She enjoyed the spirit of camaraderie of the group—her new, "friendlier" sorority—but she also relished the excitement of new tasks, and took satisfaction in doing work that mattered. She changed beds, straightened up rooms, bathed patients, filled out charts, and gave enemas, all while wearing heels that made her feet "awfully tired," but in the end she agreed with one of her fellow nurses in training who said "there is no reason why I should like it,

46

but I do." These are feelings she would return to again and again in her letters in later years, a clear sense of purpose and direction in life that brought her happiness.

She never had those feelings again.

~ ~ ~

On the night of the holiday formal, near the end of my mother's last semester before nurse's training, Dad called to tell her that he had to see her to discuss a letter his father had sent. She had not had a chance to prepare for the dance—she still had to press the gown and put up her hair—but she agreed to meet Dad early thinking that his mother, who had been seriously ill, had died.

"What did your father say?" my mother asked when she got into the car.

"Oh, he didn't say anything," Dad answered, no doubt smiling at his ruse as he handed her "the ring."

My dad did not have much money at the time. His father had struggled to make it as a rancher in Dodge City paying doctor bills for his dying wife and had little to contribute for college, so my dad took loans and drove a taxi to work his way through school. My mother said that the ring was beautiful, if modest. "Of course, it isn't large, but it has a gorgeous setting," and she immediately "had to dash back into the house to show all the girls." The night that she said "yes" my mother was happy. After dinner my newly engaged parents danced to Gene Krupa's band. "I wasn't really expecting to like his band," she wrote, but she was predisposed to enjoy the night, and when she heard Krupa play a few solos and then allow others in the band to take solos as well, she appreciated his modesty and generosity of spirit and, catching glimpses of her ring as she danced, left "completely sold" on the group—and on Dad.

~ ~ ~

47

When my dad proposed, a general destiny was sketched out, and my mother was left to work out the nettlesome details. She began by defending her marriage plans against the objections of my grandparents. They wanted her to finish nursing school and knew that a marriage would jeopardize that plan. My grandmother also believed that my dad was a "gold digger," marrying a doctor's daughter for the money. In one letter, answering that accusation which ostensibly came from a cousin, my mother wrote an angry response: "I believe that Connie's idea that Max is playing me for a sucker is not an original one—in fact I believe you once told me the same thing. Now you can imagine how much it hurt when you said that to me." She defended her future husband and assured her mother that she had not been putting on airs. "Only time will tell if Max thinks he is marrying me for my money," she wrote in an uncharacteristically incoherent sentence, adding defensively that she had not acted in a way that would lead him to think she was wealthy. "Good heavens, I don't have a fur coat, radio, or anything that would give that impression."

My mother won this battle, which meant that my dad won as well. Not being married put too much strain on the relationship. Since Dad had just started his practice in Dodge City, he always arrived in Lawrence late on Saturday, giving him and my mother little time together before her curfew. If they were married she would be able to get an apartment and see him for longer hours on his weekend visits. She also insisted that she would finish school.

"Max and I have made an agreement," she wrote confidently. "I said I wouldn't marry him now except with the understanding between us that I would go ahead and finish nurses' training." She conceded that she was asking for their advice, not insisting, but the implication of the letter was that she had made up her mind: "There comes a time when you're ready to be married. If you pass up that time your wedding becomes an anti-climax and a big disappointment."

~ ~ ~

They honeymooned at the Elms, a grand limestone hotel in Excelsior Springs near Kansas City known for its mineral waters, large grounds, and horseback riding. The corner room with large windows was, like the wedding, 'just perfect': "The windows had white Venetian blinds and gorgeous light green drapes. The bedroom suite was of very light wood—with a gorgeous green bed spread." Later in the letter my mother apologizes for using the word "gorgeous" too often, lamenting that her vocabulary was not equal to the grandeur of the hotel, but she certainly conveys her joy and excitement at being there and being married at last.

"We went riding for an hour. The road curved around the green, tree-covered hills that reminded me of the mountains in the East. We came to a white gate. A man was there so he opened it for us and we rode up the lane between two rows of trees." At dinner they had their first taste of champagne. "When the waiter brought us the drink he made quite a procedure out of pouring it into the glass." She drew a small picture of the champagne glass and wrote, that the flutes were "very different" and "delicate" with a "stem that is hollow so the champagne flows clear to the bottom." She admitted to some disappointment with the bland taste, but she was captivated by the drink anyway. "Champagne is so beautiful to look at. The bubbles keep rising to the top of the glass and form a miniature fountain."

Two weeks later, she quit the nursing program and joined Dad in Dodge City.

~ ~ ~

"I'm getting to be like a potted plant," my mother groused. "When I go outside in the afternoon I practically wilt." She had set up house, and their new place had air conditioning, a rarity then, but summer temperatures in Dodge City often rose above a hundred degrees Fahrenheit, turning the indoors into an artificial environment, a cool oasis in a hot land, and she felt the contrast whenever she entered the world. She had little experience as a housekeeper despite her nurse's training. Dad taught her how to cook by showing her the way to make each dish the first time, and he helped choose the groceries at Peterson's market in town. Mother had to clean house as well, also apparently for the first time. "I'm enjoying cooking and keeping house at present," she admitted, but added a reservation. "It won't be so much fun when the new wears off."

~ ~ ~

The most delightful and daunting surprise was the gift of Cricket, a black mare. "Last night we went out to see my horse," she wrote. "She certainly is a beautiful thing." Cricket was large, between sixteen and seventeen hands high, with a strong neck and shoulders and a deeply defined jugular groove. "She is coal black—not a white spot on her," and "shines like a million dollars." Every night that they did not have company, Mom and Dad had to drive to the stables and brush her to keep the glossy shine.

My mother was excited about the horse, but anxious as well. "I'm afraid she will throw me because I don't know how to ride." Dad had grown up in Dodge City, a western Kansas town where horses were common, but, my mother from Glen Elder to the east had little experience with them. So she started slowly, sitting on Cricket while Dad led the mare around a pen. "She isn't completely broken, but she is awfully gentle." Within a month, my mother was riding every night and, in one picture taken by a family friend, she and Dad are both on horseback, my dad in an open-necked dress shirt and my mother wearing pleated riding pants, a short-sleeved, white blouse, and gloves. She seems comfortable in the pictures as if she has found her stride in the late evening scene, the bright Kansas sky darkening behind her while the shadows of the horse barn lengthened toward the horizon.

~ ~ ~

"We rode Cricket and Princess on a ten mile ride along the creek Sunday morning," my mother wrote on September 9, 1946. She doesn't identify the creek, and I'm not sure which one since Dodge City sits above the Ogallala Aquifer, the largest underground water reservoir in the world, so spring-fed streams are abundant throughout the region. My parents may have ridden on trails along Buckner or Mulberry to the south or Saw Log and Duck to the north. The terrain would have been irregular prairie land marked by low slopes and fractured, windblown bluffs of silt and sand and sandstone. As they made their way along the stream on horseback, they would have observed a landscape where buffalo grass colors the sandy plains with low lying stretches of apple-green and mingles with the purple shades of Blue Grama, a short grass with dark-shaded, eyelash seed heads. From horseback, the largely treeless plains would have appeared as a pallet of pastels.

She exercised her horse almost every evening during the first few months in Dodge City when she and my dad rode together, learning to ride well, and the all-day adventure on horseback suggests how accomplished she had become. She knew that her choice to marry my father and give up her career meant that she would have to see her life in new ways, and a test of her willingness to adjust would be the ebony mare that waited for her every afternoon. I imagine her sitting tall in her saddle, her trim figure a silhouette against a glowing Kansas sunset, and I know that when she looked out over the scenery of western Kansas during a long ride she felt the glory of the place and endeavored to see it as home and fall in love with it and with her husband. "We rested our horses four times, and let them eat grass."

From horseback they could look out on long stretches of ranchland interrupted here and there by windbreaks of ash, elm, cottonwood, and oak. In spring, wildflowers added streaks of blue and purple to the open fields where cattle gathered at watering holes and deer hid among clumps of blooming barberry, mock orange, and privet. Crests of hills might open onto panoramic vistas of fields, prairie lands, and streams with geese in formation flying overhead and honking while seeking nightly shelter on ponds and creeks. "It's stunning," my mother wrote in letters home, looking out on a broad and desolate horizon, knowing that her words were inadequate to catch the truth.

"Gorgeous."

I see my mother as she and Dad come upon a stretch of open prairie, she "kissing" her horse awake with that clucking sound riders make and pressing her knees into the girth of the animal, as Cricket takes off full-tilt for home and hay. I hear the breathing of my mother's horse, heavy and steady and matching hers, as she leans into the animal's crest and pumps the muscular barrel chest of the mare with her legs, the mane all the while swatting her face and neck. Heading toward a narrow ravine, horse and rider become one in a sudden exhilaration as they dash away from the sun-heavy horizon in the west toward the dark of dusk, breaking free of land at each stride and racing smooth as the wind above thudding hooves toward a vanishing point forever out of reach.

~ ~ ~

Wonder Question: What is forever out of reach?

Next to the discussion of perspective in *The Book of Knowledge* is a black-and-white photograph of a straight highway heading toward the horizon of a flat landscape. The photo credit is to the "National Film Board" and the caption reads, "Where distance lends perspective to the view." I run my finger along the ribbon of road and feel the sides of the highway closing in. "If you look down the road as far as you can see, there is no width to it at all, and its two sides seem to come together in a point." My finger reaches the spot. "It is at this point that the straight lines go into the picture" and "seem to stop." But this distance, I realize, as I lift my finger and stare into the depths of the photograph, is forever out of reach. "Artists call it the vanishing point."

~ ~ ~

She began helping Dad at work, and found at first that she liked to stay busy. Her nurse's training came in handy as she assisted in the care of animals. "Max says it really helps him a lot and I love doing it. Guess I'm just a nurse at heart." She was in charge of the medications for dogs and cats, changed bandages, and administered shots, and felt "a certain satisfaction" at using her skills. They worked until 9:30 or ten each night and did not eat until after they came home when their stomachs were "really rubbing the backbone," but the pace reminded her of the excitement of her time as a student. "I'm happier now that I'm back taking care of patients." At one point she mentions that Dad paid her a salary, but dismissed the gesture as a joke saying the paycheck was just to wake him up in the morning.

Despite its intensity, though, work functioned more as a distraction from a growing emptiness than a real source of contentment, and she often mentions how much she missed school and nurse's training. "I still get a lump in my throat every time I write to the kids in training." She also worried about the lack of intellectual challenges. "Yes it is wonderful not having to study all the time, but I'm getting so lazy. I just have to push myself."

"As usual I'm pretty lonesome," she wrote after a visit to her family in Glen Elder, "but always am after I've seen you." On one trip back to Dodge City she "cried from Glen to Cawker," until Dad became concerned and had to pull over. No matter how beautiful the wind-swept prairie of western Kansas might be from horseback, it was not home.

"I guess at heart," she wrote, "I'm just a Glen Elder girl."

~ ~ ~

My mother spent a good deal of time guessing at her heart. On the envelope of one of the letters from 1947, Dad, who was fond of creating likenesses, made a line drawing of her. He used stationery from work, with "Dr. M. J. Harvey, Veterinarian" printed in the return address, so it was probably done during a lull. In it, she looks young and elegant, her hair pulled back from her face exposing a pearl earring. The mouth appears soft and relaxed, but the jaw line is firm and the eyes are odd, attentive and apprehensive at once. I hold the envelope under a light. Both alert and detached in the drawing, the face wears an expression that I find in many later photographs, but this appears to be the first time, and it comes from dad's hand like a relic placed in my care. It reveals a woman in conflict with herself.

I set the envelope on the ledge beside my computer. When did that look enter their marriage?

I cover the right side of her face with a piece of scrap paper and look at the left: her expression is animated— not happy really, but in the high arch of the eyebrow and the slight uptick of the mouth I find delight and engagement. Even the eye—which has a small worry line above the top lid looks wide open and serene, as if something has caught her attention and brought comfort. But when I cover the left side and look only at the right, her expression becomes severe, the eyebrow lowered, the smile crumbling at one edge, and the eye looking down and away with anxiety. What truth had my dad's pen caught in simple lines? What did he think when he leaned back from his handiwork, as he often did when finishing a drawing, and saw the face he had rendered looking back at him enigmatically? What did she think when he turned it to her on the counter at work? Did she laugh? And when she saw it later, as she put the envelope in her pocketbook to post, did she stop abruptly registering the underlying unease of the image without knowing exactly why?

That unease is what I sense now, as I remove the covering from the happy side of the face and look at the whole three-quarter profile again in a drawing older than myself. The look of knowledge and wonder. Yes, I think, the truth was there, for all to see, even then, and I feel her emerging woe.

Woe. The word missing from *The Book of Knowledge*.

~ ~ ~

One morning Mom had to put a tracer on a package that she sent to her mother. At the post office she described the package and its contents and filled out forms with addresses and other information—"a lot of red tape like that." The next day, while cleaning her car, she found the package under boxes of medical supplies in the trunk. Dad had forgotten to send it. "Boy, right then and there I hit the ceiling," she exclaimed. "I just don't think there is any excuse at all for a man twenty-three years old forgetting to mail a package." It upset her because my dad knew that the package was important to her and still he forgot to send it. The night did not go well. "Anyway, it ended up that I slept in the front room bed and he slept in the bed on the back porch." When I picture her angry and hurt and unable to sleep, lying alone in the dark in the bedroom and guessing long into the night at the nature of her heart, it is the Janus face of the line drawing that I see.

"Guess I'm getting in a rut," she wrote.

She had been married one year.

~ ~ ~

The differences between my mother and father eventually became unbearable, and on a weekend fishing trip to Lake Meade with a group of friends my mother stopped guessing at her heart and admitted to herself that the marriage was broken. The men fished late without catching anything, and she had to fry enough chicken to feed everyone while one of the other wives, Sue Zimmerman, watched. Sue "is very definitely not the domestic type," my mother wrote. About my mother's height, but a little thinner, Sue was a blue-eyed blonde. Like my mother she had married a gregarious and

56

talkative man and was, herself, quiet and soft-spoken, but in some ways she represented all that my mother had given up when she left college to marry Dad. "She has a good job and she said she would rather work all her life than do the housework." She is "very intelligent and nice to be with," my mother explained, and in her reserved way she offered a relief from her talkative husband. She was "exactly the opposite."

"I have just pretty well decided that opposites always marry," my mother surmised, but as she arranged the chicken in the skillet and talked with her blonde counterpart, she must have felt with full force, the trap she had set for herself by marrying Dad. Like my mother, Sue had married into this swirl, but unlike her she had managed to hold onto a bit of her independence with a job of her own and a stiff-backed refusal to cook and clean. What did my mother have to insulate herself from my father's ambitions? And if she did manage to shield herself from his gregarious ways and adventurous spirit and managed to be herself, who would she be? No doubt she turned her face to Sue at the moment of her realization, one eyebrow high and arched and the other drooping as the pan sizzled beside her.

Two weeks later, she and Dad were in counseling.

~ ~ ~

"Mother, as you know and Daddy probably you know, too, Max and I haven't been getting along too well," my mother wrote on Sunday, June 18, 1948. "Well, last Wednesday evening I gave Max quite a rude awakening to the situation." It is not hard to see what led up to this confrontation: his demanding and exhausting job, his tendency to lie and smooth over difficulties, her gloominess, her sense of failure since she had quit nurses' training and her regrets about that, her nostalgia for home coupled with the sense that she did not really feel at home in Dodge, and, above all, her sense that she and my dad were "opposites." The problems were obvious enough for her to assume that my grandfather already knew about the trouble.

The next day, my dad set up the appointment with Dr. Jackman for Friday, June 16, 1948. "He is an M.D.," my mother wrote, "but he uses a lot of psychology along with it." A quiet and sensitive physician, Dr. Jackman was "a little effeminate," as my mother put it. He refused to take sides in their arguments and seemed to care about each of them. "He is very interested in helping young people with their marriage difficulties." He was a "good listener" who spoke with a calm authority that both my mother and my dad trusted: "once he starts talking quietly and sincerely, you can't help but listen."

He spoke with each of them alone before seeing them together. When he was finished, he told both of them "frankly and in front of each other" that their "adjustment to marriage" was a "complete failure." He admonished Dad for lying about finances which did not protect my mother and only hid problems and undermined trust. He prescribed medicine for my mother's chronic sadness and suggested that she return to work at my dad's animal hospital so that she could "be near" her husband and "really become acquainted with him." He also insisted that they immediately take a week's vacation away from home and the pressures of my dad's work. "You must have a few days alone and together." When my parents explained that a vacation at that time was "impossible because of finances," Dr. Jackman remained adamant: "sell something because your marriage is at stake."

He saw potential in their marriage because, despite their differences, they "were very well suited for each other" but only if they could overcome "very dangerous difficulties." Implicit in Dr. Jackman's recommendations, I think, is the idea that my parents had become sexually distant from each other. His suggestions that they "be near" each other and become "acquainted again" and that they find "a few days alone together" sound like a prescription for a couple that has found sexual intimacy to be a problem, and his final recommendation addressed the matter bluntly.

"He thought we should start our family," my mother explained. When she and Dad told him that they both wanted children but felt they had to "postpone them because of finances," Dr. Jackman rejected the excuse again. Clearly he thought that my parents' anxiety about money was primarily a way to avoid facing the real problems: "He said if we would work together instead of against each other our finances would improve."

~ ~ ~

"Listen to this," I said to Barbara when I got to the letter. We were having coffee in the den, a bright autumn afternoon streaming through the windows. After I read it to her we both sat back. Barbara, who knew my grandmother better than I did, was surprised. She had no idea that my parents were having such difficult problems so early in their marriage. What struck me was my mother's candor.

"I can't believe she wrote all this," I said at last. "To her *mother*."

Later as I thought about it I realized that she could not hold this kind of news back. She felt alone with Dad and separated from those who would understand and sympathize. I don't think she knew how to make a close friend her own age with whom she could share these intimacies. So she was alone with a secret: she had married a man who did not understand her. He may have been a man who would come out to your farm on a snowy night to deliver a breached calf, and he also knew how to share a cigarette and talk until dawn with the customer, telling jokes and sharing stories until the animal was "out of the woods" and the farmer felt comfortable enough with the situation that he could leave. He could do all that naturally, and be honest and friendly as he swapped stories and told jokes, but he could not reach this woman who hid herself from him. The next day he would be back at work with an hour's sleep after a silent breakfast.

So it was an act of courage on my mother's part to deliver this "rude awakening" to my Dad, to break through melancholy and emerge, the soft wet skin and wings of vulnerability exposed as the arch of her being rose against the shell of their daily lives and split the protective covering wide open. The marriage may have felt accidental, but the truth is that Dad was not a stranger. They were opposites, but a part of her longed for his boldness, and in the end her deepest problem was not that my father was an ebullient and ambitions man, but that she was a stranger to her own capacity for joy. Awakening was her only recourse, shattering the night with a scream, a thrown tumbler, and an outburst of words spoken at last, stiff, arthropodal words, humped and gooey and segmented, emerging like a gasp for air.

~ ~ ~

After talking with the counselor, Dad tried, with occasional slips, to walk the hard plank of telling the truth, though the old habit of obfuscation was difficult to break: "He stumbles once in a while," my mother wrote, "but immediately corrects himself—he is trying very, very hard and I am too." My mother attempted to shed her dark thoughts about their life together. "Max and I are happy for the first time since our marriage," she announced triumphantly, and she added that her friends could already tell a difference in her. She writes, cryptically, that the "marriage relationship has already been corrected," probably a veiled way of indicating to her mother that she and my dad were having sex again. She ends the letter with a P.S.: "I love my husband very, very much and he also feels the same way. *Oh! It is a happy day.*"

~ ~ ~

My parents' problems appeared to recede like objects on the horizon behind them. "We're having a wonderful two-day vacation," my mother wrote on a postcard from Pike's Peak in Colorado. The card is a colorized view of the mountains showing the parallel lines of a switchback road leading up to a snow-covered mountain and meeting at the top. White cumulus clouds glow in an azure sky with a hint of a yellow sunset at the horizon. "We've really kept busy seeing the sights," Mom added. "We're on the Peak now."

By the end of October, my mother thought she was pregnant. "I'm pretty sure now," she wrote, and planned to see the doctor. "Keep your fingers crossed," she added hopefully. In December my mother had a date: "Baby to be born around June 15. Mother feeling wonderful. Hasn't been sick a day." In January my mother went shopping in Meade for maternity dresses with her friend Eathel but couldn't find anything to buy. "Eathel was kidding me that I didn't like them because they made me look pregnant," she joked. At her monthly check-up, Dr. Jackman mentioned that she would "be feeling movement any time now." She seemed to have more energy and assured her mother that it was no chore to entertain houseguests. "I sometimes even forget I'm pregnant until I walk in front of a mirror."

~ ~ ~

But the problems did not go away and the letters are a thin veil over my mother's growing fear and anxiety. She and my dad took Dr. Jackman's advice to get away, but they went for a long weekend rather than a week, violating the spirit of the trip by using finances once again as an excuse. The postcard folded in with the letter does offer a view of the mountains at sunset under white clouds, but when I follow the parallel lines of a switchback road leading up to the snow-covered peak I think of their perpetually tandem but separate lives, and even with colorization, the scene looks desolate, a broken road to nowhere vanishing on an isolated mountain top.

In the third month of her pregnancy, a blizzard struck western Kansas and Dodge City. The newspaper reported 800 missing, many of them, including my dad, stranded in cars on the side of the road. He and a friend, Mac McAllister, were on a call near Fowler, a town about thirty-five miles away from home. It was snowing when they left at one o'clock, but no one suspected a blizzard. At 11:15 my mother finally called in a report, but she did not learn until 1:15 that her husband was safe at a farmhouse. The men had gotten stuck in a drift ten miles outside of town. Mac had a condition that required he eat often, but he and my dad had no water and only a Hershey bar between them. "Max said Mac vomited what he had in his stomach and then would try to vomit without any results."

Clippings from newspapers describe hotel lobbies filling with the stranded who spent the night trapped. "As the long-awaited dawn cracked through the ghostly white atmosphere," one paper reported poetically, "tired faces turned gray in its light." The storm disrupted communications and blocked roads throughout southwest Kansas. By the second day there were five known fatalities, including Maxine Laughlin, a thirty-year-old woman from Jetmore who tried to escape the blizzard by car with her seventy-five-year-old mother-in-law. When the car stalled, Maxine attempted to get help on foot, but after trudging a mile or so she collapsed and began crawling. It took the recovery team a day to locate her body which was "found in a kneeling position" under a five foot drift, her legs bruised and bloody. She was eight months pregnant.

~ ~ ~

In the last days of 1948, six months from my birth, my parents' neighbor, Wilson Lane, killed himself in his car which was parked near the Ford County Lake. He died of carbon monoxide poisoning and police called the death a suicide. My mother learned this news from another neighbor before Dad got home from work, but could not bring herself to visit Lane's wife Rose who was her friend. "I've heard so many, many rumors why he committed suicide that I wouldn't know which, if any, were true," my mother wrote anxiously. Outwardly, he had "everything to live for," including three sons and a "secure job at Combs Automotive Company."

In the letter she speculates on her own mental state and her reluctance to help. "I was nervous and upset," she admitted. Being "nervous" was her euphemism for attacks of anxiety just as feeling "tired" was code for depression. Both were becoming more of a problem for her. "Usually I'm calm about such things, but since I've been pregnant I tire quicker and get nervous."

After the New Year, my mother's friend Margaret had a miscarriage when she fell on the stairs. "She and

Stan are practically sick with grief," Mother wrote. "I said they shouldn't feel too bad—surely they'll have another if they could have one." Still my dad cautioned that my mother had better not visit for a few days because Margaret was for the moment inconsolable: "when she sees a pregnant woman," Dad explained, "she bursts into tears."

I arrived on June 9, 1949. "People have been dropping in all week to see Steven," my mother declared, adding that it had been "awfully hard" to get her "naps in." Soon she brought me home where her parents had arrived to help. When I cried, they had calmed me with long rides in their Chrysler, and my grandpa regaled me with faces and antics to get me to smile. It didn't work. "Steven smiles now," my mother wrote in her first letter home two months after my birth. "Too bad he didn't do that sooner when you folks were here."

"What happened to the woman I married?" is the kind of question my dad would have asked because he was a charmer and an optimist by nature and did not understand a disease so embedded in the psyche as to be without a cure. He was the kind of man who thought every problem could be solved with hard work, a winning smile, and a firm handshake because he had solved so many that way. His eyes never caught up with her darkness. The woman who shopped for black negligees, danced late into the night, ate barbecue cooked on a spit on the side of the road, was, in fact, a mirage. She preferred sedate music to flashy jazz tunes, thought the musicians looked odd, and quickly retreated to the balcony when the dance floor got crowded, watching from the edges in her stocking feet. KC was Dad's scene, not hers, and I don't know if my dad ever figured that out. What happened to the woman he married?

She was never that woman.

What he did not realize is that she had felt compelled, since her childhood, to stay at the edges. She withheld herself from the social whirl and was often brooding and meditative. In part, her reserve was the result of her Kansas upbringing where reticence was prized in girls, and she was expected to be the small town doctor's perfect daughter. But the darkening of the mind that caused her to retreat goes deeper than that, eventually causing her to recoil entirely from life, and it can be traced back to the doctor himself.

~   ~   ~

Almost every summer when I was growing up my mother would take my brother and me to Glen Elder, Kansas to stay at my grandparents' house. We would board the train in Chicago, and for hours I sat beside the window watching Illinois go by in a blur. When we arrived in Salina, my grandparents would be at the platform, Grandpa thin and tidy in his wire-rimmed glasses and fedora and Grandma plump and pleasant in a flower-print dress. When she hugged me she smelled like powder and mints.

My grandfather married my grandmother in 1922 after she graduated from high school in a simple home ceremony, the bride wearing "a white crepe de chine dress decorated with white bugle beads." They moved into the house in Glen Elder and spent their honeymoon redecorating the long and narrow bungalow where they would live for the next forty years. Four years after they married, my grandmother gave birth to a baby girl who would become my mother. Named "Roberta" after my grandfather, she went by "Bobbie," but sometimes used the boy's spelling "Bobby" for her nickname. *The History of Kansas*, volume 5, of the American Historical Society, published in 1928, describes her as a "winsome little daughter."

Life in Glen Elder seemed idyllic when we made our annual summer visit: hot suppers in mid-day, horses in the school yard across the street, fireworks on the Fourth of July in the spot behind the house where several backyards met, and Sunday services at the Methodist church. My grandfather was well known by everyone in town as the friendly doctor with a calm manner who told funny stories. He made house calls until a stroke forced him to retire. My mother was also well-liked and, based on those who fussed over my brother and me and often leaned over to confide in us, had once been the darling of the little town and was often written about in the paper. In fact, our arrival "to visit the home of Dr. and Mrs. Robert Reinhardt" always made the newspaper as well.

I admired my soft-spoken and thoughtful grandfather. Without warning, he could pull a silver dollar out of my ear and hand it to me as a gift, and he seemed to have an endless supply as part of his coin collection which included a cardboard display of wheat pennies that I admired, too. He could also recite the names of the Presidents of the United States from memory, a feat that brought endless delight to me, especially the part when he dutifully repeated the name of the only president who served two non-consecutive terms: ". . . Chester A. Arthur, Grover Cleveland, Benjamin Harrison, Grover Cleveland. . . ." I bugged my grandfather continually to repeat the list the way some children ask for a favorite story or song, making a pest of myself. It had a lovely lilt and rhythm to it—on his lips it was poetry—and no sooner did he finish than I would vow, yet again, to learn it myself and got about as far as Franklin Pierce or Zachary Taylor before the poetry turned to putty, and I quit, disgusted with myself. Once, when I wondered aloud how my grandfather could learn so many Presidential names, my Dad laughed and said that he had probably voted against half of them.

~ ~ ~

So in part to keep me from asking again, my family thought that I should spend time with his brother, my Uncle Henry, the Reinhardt boy who did not become a doctor, could not recite a list of Presidents, collected days instead of coins, and spent his mornings fishing for mudcat in the Solomon River. I was sent with a lunch basket for the two of us and told to stand on the sidewalk in front of the house, where Uncle Henry would pick me up, usually by driving his truck over the curb and often nearly running me down. That was the other reason they sent me to fish with Henry. He couldn't see well enough to drive, and I was to be his eyes.

"Watch for a gravel road to the left," Henry would say. "Right about...."

"That road?" I'd ask.

Suddenly Henry would yank the wheel and downshift, sometimes crunching the stones dead on, sometimes taking out some grass and dirt, but always close enough. Once we ran up a log and the truck nearly spun off the road, Henry fishtailing across the gravel until he got his pickup under control.

It was an adventure.

Henry didn't really need me or my eyes, of course. He often made the trip alone and, blind merely to the world, always found the fish. Glen Elder, an oasis of trees, lies amid the fields of wheat and milo that stretch to the Kansas horizon and fill the eye, creating a kind of blindness of abundance for the sighted, the dizziness of being nowhere and everywhere at once. We rarely met another car or truck on the road, and my eyes offered little help, but Henry, unfazed by the vertigo of an undifferentiated landscape, knew the way by the feel of the road and the lay of the land under the pickup's tires. He had long ago given up going to church and liked to spend his Sundays, like all of his days, beside a stream. Fish, the focus of his devotion, lay in wait at the other end of this dusty stretch, and he went after them by faith—yes, blind faith to be sure—but faith grounded in years of farming land that he knew by heart.

The only time I ever saw my grandfather angry was after a confrontation at Uncle Henry's funeral. I'm not sure how old I was when Henry died, but I imagine I was about ten, old enough for the scene that followed to make an impression. During his homily, the minister must have made a joke about the fact that this was the first time in years that Henry, who lay in repose at the altar, had been *in* a church, a crack that infuriated my grandfather who apparently broke the Kansas custom of saying nothing in public about matters of importance and let the minister have a piece of his presidentially endowed mind on the church steps.

We had stony silence in the house after that, my grandfather in the parlor undoing his tie and my mother and grandmother setting out supper.

"He should have said nothing about it," my grandfather muttered. "If he had any decency he would have kept his mouth shut."

"And so should you," my grandmother snapped in retort. That of course was the end of it. This was Kansas, after all, where the rest *is* silence.

~ ~ ~

In company my grandfather was witty and entertaining and could tell funny tales. A Democrat in a house of Republican women, especially my strong-willed grandmother, he had to hold his own. Once he asked, as a favor, for my grandmother to vote for FDR, and she agreed, but later confided that when she went into the polling booth she just could not bring herself to pull the lever for a Democrat. He also liked to recite Bible stories and tales from Uncle Remus and read to me from books, his voice soft and gravelly, barely, but meaningfully, animated with meaning. I may not be able to hear my mother's voice any more, but the rasp of my grandfather's speech remains in the mind: "Chester A. Arthur, Grover Cleveland, Benjamin Harrison, Grover Cleveland." Knowing the script helps.

In the end, though, when I think of summers in Kansas and my grandfather, I think of the cicada hum of unspoken words. Sometimes, after evening fell and the women had slipped back inside the house to do the dishes, my grandfather would sit alone in the darkening landscape, wearing his pleated slacks, dress shirt, suspenders, vest, and a short tie that came about half-way down his shirt front. Usually he held a newspaper in his lap, or passed a coin mindlessly through his fingers, and just looked off. The house was in town on a quiet street across from an elementary school and an open field, where light rays descending on the prairie shimmered through different layers of air, as he sat in the porch swing that faced the side yard, his eyes not really registering what was around him, his mind lost in thought. After he had his stroke—and his speech came slowly and slurred—the silence was more profound, and in it I heard the unasked questions, unmet needs, and unspoken doubts of a reticence that he shared with my mother.

I have many pictures of my grandfather with my mother, and in all of them he wears a kind face with a quizzical half smile. Even after his stroke, when one cheek sagged a bit altering his appearance, the smile remained unchanged because it had always been a little bent at one corner. Like my mother, he enjoyed fine clothes, especially woolen suits and vests. He almost always wore formal attire and has on a shirt and tie in every photograph I have except for a few of his fishing trips, and even then, he kept the shirt buttoned to the top

70

or wore a bandanna at his neck. As a young man he had broad features: wide set eyes, a long nose, a sensual mouth and strong chin, and olive skin like my mother's that became soft and craggy when he was old. His hair gradually went from brown to gray, thinning on the sides, and, when I remember him best, it was pure white. The pictures record his changing appearance, but it is that wry smile that remains constant, so that in each photo he looks a little startled, a little out of place, as if surprised at the attention and caught off guard.

That is the way I, pushing the letters and pictures aside and recalling the man from memory, remember him on those Kansas evenings. I would climb into the porch swing beside him, and he would look away from whatever in his inward gaze held his attention, and look down at me, a little startled that I would just climb in the swing that way knocking papers awry and causing the seat to teeter on its chains. I don't think he was ever completely at home in the world of others. He may have been social and funny and entertaining when he had to be, but he was the kind of man who was most himself when alone, and therefore something of a puzzle to those who loved him. When I scooted beside him, and he set down his paper, and put his hand around my shoulder, he knew what I wanted, and was happy to please me, but looking back now I sense that he left the world of his thoughts—his brooding, melancholy musings—reluctantly as he began with a sigh his solo recitation: "George Washington, John Adams, Thomas Jefferson, James Madison, James Monroe, John Quincy Adams…."

~ ~ ~

The family secret was that my grandfather suffered from depression, a deep and abiding melancholy that was the source of my mother's predisposition to the disease.

In a brief autobiographical statement that she wrote before her death, my grandmother does not mention his depression, creating a blind spot in the formal record and suggesting just how sensitive the topic was with her, but in a rough draft of the statement that she included in papers left to me she does write the truth before having second thoughts and crossing it out, adding a crucial link to the story of my mother. It is easy to read what she had hoped to hide. After his stroke on the Friday before Christmas in 1955, my grandfather was "very depressed and was in hospitals in Beloit, Concordia, Salina, and Halstead without too much success." The long list of hospitals shows how desperate he and my grandmother were for relief, and foreshadows my grandparents' futile attempts to get help for my mother, especially the last time when her depression turned suicidal. It was not until one of his doctors prescribed Thorazine, an anti-psychotic drug synthesized in the fifties, that my grandfather improved, and even then he could be morose.

This gloom created an intuitive connection between my mother and my grandfather. They had experienced feelings of shared pain when she was younger, my mother explained in one letter, suggesting that the melancholy they suffered was longstanding. She believed it was a psychic link that grew stronger as she got older allowing them to sense each other's pain even over great distances. On the night of his stroke in 1955, she felt a passing sensation of dread which she took as an omen. "On Friday," she wrote, "I had a feeling come over me in the bedroom." She described it as "a moment of either being scared or uneasy" that caused her to leave the bedroom and tell my father about it. "I did have that feeling," she insisted marveling at the uncanny experience because her father was in Kansas and she in New York. "It is amazing with all the miles between us we would still know something had happened to make us uneasy." This sympathetic bond was mutual. It was my grandfather, after all, who first sensed something wrong with my mother, despite her upbeat letters in 1953, a time she later described as her "year of blackness." He knew what was wrong because he recognized it in himself. Her use of the word "us" in describing the feeling is odd and telling: "something had happened to make *us* uneasy." In her mind, they had been made soul mates by their pain, their separate personalities twisted into a single strand of darkness that reached halfway across a continent. That tie of shared emotions may explain why my grandfather died of a heart attack within three weeks of my mother's suicide. Her pain may have been too heavy a burden for him to bear and her death may have dug a hole in his life that he could not fill.

I think of him, the friendly family physician, on the porch swing, the setting sun golden on his face, staring off into the side yard, listening to something far off in the tymbalous moan of summer cicadas, something not human, something ominous. It is a dreamy tendency my mother shared, to withdraw into some cramped crawl-space of her mind, lit by the stars of her imaginings, and, drained of their melancholy and darkness of spirit, it has lodged in me too taking the shape of the writer who waits in silence, staring off toward the wall, until words form. We have formed an alliance, the three of us, the one who pondered, the one who took her life, and the one tasked with writing it all down. A vow of silence that my father despite his charm could not penetrate. The day I told my father I wanted to be a writer we were standing beside his work bench. This was some time after he had retired. He was twisting wire on a spool with his sharp-nosed pliers, tidying up, and he stopped and looked at me. "Beware what you wish for" he said, skeptically. "It will probably come true."

He was calling me back to his world, a world of practical success, a world of action, a world away from my mother and grandfather. I suspect that Dad called and called to my mother, too, but she was in so deep he could not call her back, her eyes participating in that inhuman thing, seduced by its dangers and animated by its fears, but appearing empty to him. Beware what you wish for. In Dodge City when she sat across from him in silence, the empty eyes that looked back without making contact came from her father who liked to gaze at the tree-lined horizon of the home she had missed so desperately. When my dad captured her Janus eyes in a line drawing it was my grandfather's gaze that the pencil recorded. My mother bore the disease as a legacy. It had lodged within her early, even as a girl, and though she, like my grandfather, could appear friendly and at times fun-loving and gregarious, the disease haunted them and eventually destroyed them.

That was the woman my dad married.

~ ~ ~

No summer in Kansas was complete without a trip to Waconda Springs, the shimmering pool of water in the middle of the open prairie as ephemeral in memory as a mirage. It was my grandfather's treat. Getting plastic figurines of dinosaurs and balsa gliders at the five-and-dime, tramping from house to house with the Eberly boy to gather stories for the local paper, swimming in the public pool in Beloit, feeding windfall apples to the horses across the street, and fishing for mudcat with Henry—that just about exhausts the list of things for a visiting grandson to do in and about Glen Elder. By default, the trip to the wonder of nature at the outskirts of town became the summer highlight.

Waconda was a remarkable salt water pool fed by an underground source deep in the Dakota sandstone. It was also a tourist trap. The name, given by Kansas Indians, means "spirit water," and many Midwestern tribes traveled to the spot to enjoy its healing properties. Legends naturally grew up around the pond. My brother and I read about them each year in the Waconda gift shop where racks of postcards, amid leather pouches, feathered headdresses, cap guns, and strung beads made in Japan, told the tales. According to one legend a princess pining for her lover threw herself into the waters, giving them medicinal qualities. In another, animals held council in a lodge in the pond's depths. Young braves could dive in and swim down in the hopes of learning magic from beasts gathered there.

As we waited for my grandfather to buy us *genuine* Western wallet kits that had to be stitched together with strips of plastic, we would read these magical stories. Several versions of the Indian princess legend were available on the cards and, as a sign posted beside the pond explained, Kansas senator Samuel C. Pomeroy once explored this area as a young man, declaring Waconda Springs "a most wonderful and marvelous sight." Based on the black-and-white photos I have, it really did not look like much—a salty circular pond about as wide as a football field is long surrounded by Kansas wheat. After buying our tourist booty and paying a fee, we stepped outside into the blazing sunlight and walked the little trail that led from the hotel to the pool of water, set up for disappointment by tales and toys and garishly painted signs.

And yet, the sight *was* marvelous to me then, shimmering before my eyes in the heat of the Kansas prairie with enough ambiguity to fulfill my wishes, and its memory still fills me with wonder. I was drawn to the blue surface, cool and serene and set apart from the endless wheat fields that surrounded it. As I approached, clutching the penny that my grandfather had given me tightly in one hand, I felt power emanating from some source far beyond us. As my brother and I made our way to the fenced area to toss in our coins, we looked hard for the bones of the dead princess and the animal council deep in those turquoise waters, but had trouble seeing past our own faces and the flecks of white cirrus clouds reflected there. The reflection of my grandfather standing behind us, wearing his dark fedora and glasses, looked over our shoulders into the water as well. It is the memory I most associate with him, his downward gaze deep into the pool at our feet. The lenses of his glasses catch the sun, hiding his glance for a moment, but he also seems to be looking for something down there where the bones of a princess lay. No badger rose to the surface to take our coins after we tossed them on a wish into the air, but we felt that they were headed to some place of dark enchantment as they flipped and glinted in the green depths of the pond and disappeared into the paws of oblivion.

One other feature of the springs captivated me even more than the legends associated with the place. It was an idea, a simple, and later I discovered untrue, idea that is linked with my grandfather as an eerie presence in my imagination: The pond had no bottom.

"At first I declared it the Crater of an Ancient Volcano," Senator Pomeroy wrote. "The water occupying its hollow center is fathomless."

"Fathomless" may be the very word my grandfather used as he knelt between my brother and me and pulled us to him, describing the depth of the pond in the stately and authoritative tones of an infallible physician. Some say it rises and falls with the tides of the ocean, he told us. Others say it snakes its way to the center of the planet.

"Who knows," my grandfather would add with a sardonic smile. "It may go to China."

China! My brother and I looked at him, then each other, and finally gazed deep into the waters, trying to see past the implacable surface before us to the other side of the world. Years later when the federal government put in a dam, the Army Corps of Engineers drained the pond and flooded the Solomon River basin, creating Waconda Lake. Before the flood, scuba divers were dispatched to determine Waconda Spring's source. All of us in Glen Elder were pulling for fathomlessness, but the excavation revealed that the pond did have a bottom some 800 feet below the surface. No lodge for an animal council was found, and China, the engineers explained, was never at the other end. Case closed.

But wonder *was* there, and a glory that the tacky gift shop, the cheap trinkets, the Army Corps of Engineers, and even the desecration of a Pawnee holy site could not remove. Wonder and depth and darkness. In memory, I look past the reflection of my face and my brother's and see, above our images, the image of my grandfather in the gloom joined by my mother's blurry shape when she walked up behind us at the pool's edge, putting an arm around her father. Our bodies are backlit by a nimbus of sunlight glinting in the water and our faces, especially my grandfather's half hidden by the brim of his fedora, look murky.

~ ~ ~

When my wife and I started our own family many years after my childhood summers in Glen Elder, we lived in Charlotte, North Carolina in a rented house not far from the town where her family lived. I remember one weekend walking downtown with Barbara and our baby, Matt, when I was suddenly struck by the sight of standing water in a birdbath beside a church. I was holding Matt and only paused while Barbara had pulled ahead, but I remember being for that instant frozen in place while I watched sunlight play along dark reddish scum. Leaves and gum wrappers choked the pool and some twigs, half in and half out of the water, looked bent by refraction, but what held my gaze was the creamy surface completely still that wrapped my darkened face and a bit of Matt's cap in a golden nimbus, at the same time that the slowly twisting shapes of oak leaves submerged in the shallow basin seemed to open up on an illusion of great, ever-darkening depths. Fathomlessness in six inches of muddy water.

It was one of those moments that recur in my life when I think I am in the presence of something otherworldly, far beyond the ordinary life we lead, times that I have come to associate with my mother. I did not understand then what it meant. I was simply held by the sight, having to shake my head to escape its pull, but I knew it was important. It was an eye, opening into my normal world and humdrum life, a vestige of the pool of darkness I saw with my grandfather and my mother at Waconda Springs, bequeathed to me by them, though it lay harmless between the high-rises of a city made of steel and glass.

~ ~ ~

Wonder Question: Where are all the people who have been and gone?

It was one of Marjorie Mee's original questions, coming right after "why am I here?" and giving birth to *The Book of Knowledge* with its many wonder questions. This one, though, is too hard and was left out of the book. Where *are* all the people who have been and gone? The distinguished editors won't touch it. But I know part of the answer from the pictures that my grandmother took of the graveside services conducted separately for my mother and grandfather on the open prairie of Kansas. They were, I think, my grandmother's answer to Marjorie's hard question.

One of them shows my mother's and grandfather's graves side by side. Beware what you wish for, I think rummaging through the wicker basket until I find the picture. In it my grandfather's grave is showered in ribbons and fresh roses and carnations on a bed of lush greenery with a small plastic marker bearing his name and dates as well as the name of the funeral home. My mother's has a similar spray of flowers but it lacks the marker, the carnations are wilted and in disarray, and much of the greenery is gone or dispersed showing the damage of exposure to Kansas wind and sun in the three weeks since her death. It is a heartbreaking irony, this double gravesite, recorded dutifully by my grandmother who is missing in all of the funeral pictures. She couldn't resist recording for posterity just how suddenly she was abandoned by those she loved. I imagine her looking down into the viewfinder of the Brownie held against her black crepe de chine dress, her hands steady, feeling empty and bereft, and the absence spreads out from there into the emptiness of the Kansas grassland.

My grandmother eventually remarried her old high school boyfriend and lived the happiest years of her life, I think, with him in a small apartment in Beloit, Kansas, until he died of emphysema. She found a way to survive and move on and be there for my brother and me; that in my mind is heroic. She was the keeper of my mother's story, but being forgotten is what my mother wanted. My mother feared that the darkening of spirit she carried would lead to the destruction of those that she loved. And here is where I enter the story again, along with my brother. Just as she thought she had inherited her illness from her father, so, she believed, would she pass on her illness to her children, and all of the love she could muster would not stop the ugly and inevitable cycle. I imagine her on the morning of my birth looking at me for early signs. I wish I could tell her, as I let the photograph of the graves drop from my fingers and set aside the looking glass, that it never happened. I wish my voice could reach back in time to say the legacy stopped with her. But I can't. On the day of my birth, when the nurses aren't looking, she studies my hands and feet, my genitals, and she seeks out any rashes along my neck and arms for clues that my grandfather within her would show up somewhere in me. And she studies my eyes. That is where the truth will emerge, in the blue pools lodged in the baby's face. She looks deep into my eyes with the same intensity that my brother and I brought to the pool at Waconda, searching for swimming beasts in the stew and fearing that her children, like her, were cursed the day they were born.

~ ~ ~

Where are all the people who have been and gone?

I lift the picture of their graves one last time. In the foreground, the two heaps of flowers look like an aberration, especially my grandfather's funeral spray which is some kind of collection of tender and vibrant life heaped high, arranged symmetrically, and quivering in the wind, but my mother's grave serves as a reminder of where this tribute to his life is headed as the brown earth of the dug grave on her side of the divide is exposed here and there by the rotting and scattering of the greens and blossoms. The arrangement itself seems to snake along the ground in a line of ragged clumps with the ribbons missing altogether, blown away on their winged bows and long gone. She got her wish. By killing herself suddenly, she snipped a clean break in the line of succession, making the two graves look even more lonely somehow as they become the gloom that they alone share forever.

In 1950 my dad acquired a job with Lederle laboratories of American Cyanamid as a managing director of field work, an experiment involving the testing and promoting of new products. He would contact veterinarians who were willing to participate in the experiment, guaranteeing any losses, to test whether the vaccines were effective. If the products were successful, the veterinarians would know and recommend the product to farmers. Dad's job was to act as the middleman between the vets and the company, a task he was well suited for since he was a veterinarian himself and very effective in dealing with people. His pay was $7,200 a year—a big increase over what his practice in Dodge City was bringing in at the time—and, as my mother wrote, he was "starting on the ground floor with great possibilities for advancement." He told my mother that he thought it was the "chance of a lifetime" and she agreed. "It will take lots of work and ability, but I have confidence in Max and will back him by cooperating fully in selling this practice and helping him try his wings in experimental field work."

The "heartbreaker," as my mother put it, was that Lederle was in Pearl River, New York, just outside of the

City. She explained to her parents that she would be able to return to Kansas for vacations and that she hoped that they would be willing to spend their vacations in the East with her and her new family. She mentioned that Pearl River is "a resort town at the bottom of Bear Mountain" that is small enough to be friendly, a pitch designed to sell her parents—and, ultimately, herself—on the move. But there is a telling passivity to her description of this decision. "Plans are being made for us to move," she writes as if forces beyond her control were at work. She admits that "the one thing that is so hard is that we will be so far away," the repetition of the word "so" offering a clue to her anxiety. She never mentions any possibilities for herself or excitement about living near New York, or even about getting away from Dodge City which had never felt like home. Instead she sounds detached, even dazed, in the letter, echoing robotically my father's abstractions about advancement and his clichés about opportunity, while choking up on the real heartbreak of moving so far away from her Kansas home.

My mother may have supported Dad as he tried his "wings," but she was the shadow of them gliding along the ground.

~ ~ ~

They rented a house in Nanuet, a small town near Pearl River and Dad had begun his work at Lederle testing and promoting Rovac, a hog cholera vaccine. One of the brochures produced by Lederle has a photograph of an enormous mother hog lying on her side with eleven piglets sucking at teats. The caption says "Stop Hog Cholera—Save them all." Dad's job, which came at the initial stage of production, was to hire a team of veterinarians and begin making contacts with other vets across the country and in South America, encouraging them to use the product. "Max will be in and out quite a lot now because they hope to put Rovac on the market," my mother wrote. The work involved travel to California and the Midwest as well as to Venezuela and Brazil. Dad was sometimes gone for as much as a month at a time. In one letter, my mother joked that she had become a "travel widow."

While he was away, Mom threw herself into fixing up her new suburban bungalow, explaining that she "did a little spring housecleaning" during her first year there. She "waxed the floor with paste wax, scratched paint off windows, and washed them." She bought furniture at this time including a three-piece set of a sofa with chairs that were the backdrop of so many photos from my childhood. "It is modern," my mother explained, "and has a rounded white square figure on the seat and back of chair and divan." She mentioned that they probably got a bargain on it because the design was unconventional, but she and Dad thought it was "striking" and liked it.

On November 9, 1952, my brother, Ron, was born. There are no letters announcing the birth since my grandmother was in New York with my mother at the time to help, but "Ronnie" appears for the first time eating Pablum, having regular "bm's," and getting fussy in the afternoons in a November 26 letter.

This was my mother's new world and for the first two years she apparently adapted well enough. "We have met several couples from the plant," she wrote when she first arrived, "and have found them nice and friendly." Since the company was actively hiring fresh talent, there was "quite a nice group of younger couples." Mom and Dad began attending and hosting cocktail parties, a staple of the emerging corporate culture, the leftovers of nuts, crackers, and watery drinks that often greeted me on the weekend mornings of my childhood beginning at this time. But this contentment was temporary, and by 1953, a pall fell over my mother's world as she entered a year-long depression, a time when her former joys were draped in a shroud and the look in the eyes of the baby boy in her arms filled her with terror.

~   ~   ~

"I take a shower to wake up," my mother wrote on November, 23, 1953 "because morning is my bad time." After the first few years in New York, she often complained that the house in Nanuet was dirty and that she did not have the energy to clean it. The "social whirl" of Lederle, which had seemed so lively and youthful and exciting when she first arrived in the East had, in her mind, turned petty and ugly. Soon she dreaded the parties, which included department heads and supervisors. She called the month of March a "mad rush" as she and my dad tried to "pay back" all of their "entertainment debts" which became a bleak burden to her. The parties that she and Dad threw simply resulted in invitations to more parties given by others, the cycle perpetuating itself. "It has been a rushing month, and I still owe people," she complained. "Oh me!"

The word "rush" here means more than busy in this context. These parties were meant to impress the bosses as a way to advance in the company, an activity that my mother dismissed as "apple-polishing." Speaking of the wives of the men in my father's division, she wrote that "most of the girls in the veterinary group have been rushing both Mrs. Burkhart and Mrs. Brackett with luncheons and bridge and dinner." She detested the practice as fulsome and demeaning. "Max and I have discussed this at some length many times," she wrote as she struggled to keep her cascading bouts of anxiety and depression in check. "I told Max that I didn't feel up to it, because I was just getting on my feet and besides, even if I felt like it, I didn't believe in apple-polishing."

As it turns out, my mother's approach worked, and Dad was the one who got the first promotion out of the veterinary group. Still, she recognized her reclusiveness as a problem. "On the apple-polishing thing I don't mean to sound like I was right because I know that this is a fault of mine." She admitted that her malaise had made my father's "past year quite hard on him." It had also alienated her from possible friends: "sometimes I carry the anti-apple polishing to an extreme and people think I don't like them." She struggled to overcome her awkwardness in public, trying to "mingle" with ones "a little more poised" than she, and looking back several years later wrote, "I try to observe and learn with each experience—particularly the art (or talent, if lucky) of friendly, easy conversation."

But these attempts to become socially engaged were studied and unspontaneous. They had about them the autodidactic earnestness of a reader of *The Book of Knowledge*, and they did not work because the gloom that rose in her like a black beast had a source beyond mere lack of sociability. She found it unleashed within her during introspective moments, and it clawed its way into the open when she fought furiously with my father. Although she enjoyed her children, she admitted to being inappropriately snarly with them occasionally. "I get tired and cross sometimes." In 1953, her letters, which used to come once or twice a week, trickled down to one or two a month as she withdrew in silence from the world. When my grandmother complained about the lack of response and lectured her on her attitude, my mother wrote that she was "ashamed of her faults" but she seemed to be hiding something and for the first time rejected my grandmother as a confidante.

Her most reliable friend was the TV, which did not ask questions. Television was new in 1952, much of Kansas did not have it yet, but in New York my mother could get seven channels clearly and passed the time watching news coverage of events such as the Eisenhower inaugural and the Estes Kefauver hearings or musical specials like *Peter Pan*. With my dad traveling for weeks at a time, the TV became a companion. "I'm not much of a gad about—rather like my own home," she conceded. "I'm afraid I would be very lonely in the evenings without television."

Fortunately, our neighbor's thirteen-year-old daughter named Jean (Mom sometimes spells it as Jeanne or Jeanie) became attached to our family that summer. Jean had suffered from rheumatoid arthritis as a child and had trouble keeping up with older children in sports. Instead, she would join my mother for lunch when my dad was on trips and take my brother for a stroll while I tagged along, giving my mom a break. She became our regular babysitter and often came by in the evening to help with the baths. My mother called her a "godsend" admitting that she needed the lift: "I was so tired there for a while."

My mother lost weight, dropping down to 105 pounds, and in a letter home blamed the weight loss on a cold, but that seems unlikely. By now she was clearly shading the truth. She admitted that she hadn't been answering all of her mother's letters, and the ones she did write during the first half of the year sound listless and resigned and unusually vague. My dad bought her a suit to "cheer her up" before he left on a trip to Brazil, but though she loved clothes she expressed little enthusiasm about it, and even her customary words about longing for home sound perfunctory: "I wish I were close enough to visit you, but it is a long way."

~ ~ ~

At the end of April, my mother confessed the truth. The problem was my brother's eyes. My grandfather with his mysterious connection to my mother sensed her distress, and his growing apprehension about her led to this admission. "I was amazed when you wrote that Daddy was concerned about me because I have been upset." When my brother was four months old, my mother noticed that his eyes turned in, especially when he looked at his hands. This condition would lead to myriad trips to the doctors and two operations over the next three years which triggered a year-long period of depression in my mother. It also meant that she did not want to take any pictures of my brother until the eye problem had been cleared up.

The first eye specialist, Dr. MaGee in Hackensack, said that Ron did not have a squint, the technical term for crossed eyes, but was having trouble focusing, a condition that would heal itself over time. My mother must have expressed skepticism, or at least hinted at disappointment with the diagnosis, because the doctor felt compelled to reassure her: "As we walked out he said I will never lie to you." But my mother was convinced from the beginning that the eyes were crossed and the problem would be difficult to correct. On these points she was right. "I am," she wrote to my grandmother, "a realistic person with a little touch of pessimism."

When the squint persisted into the summer, Dr. MaGee recommended a patch. He tested Ron and found that both eyes had turned in, the left more than the right. The sight and focus was good in them, which ruled out the earlier diagnosis, but they moved independently. "Ronnie was using one eye to look one way and the other to look the other way." He was to wear the patch over one eye for one week and on the other eye the next. By alternating this way the doctor hoped to strengthen both eyes over time. When they saw the patch, several of my mother's friends said that the eyes of their children had been corrected that way, which reassured her.

Unfortunately, the patch did not work, so at the beginning of 1954, my father consulted with colleagues at Lederle to get the name of a surgeon to conduct the first set of operations. Dr. Berke began by taking measurements of Ron's eyes. He found that the left eye turned up, especially at the outside corner. To correct the problem, he would need to operate on the right eye, doing two procedures and perhaps a third over the course of three or four days to bring it up a bit to match the left eye. On the way home my mother thought about the doctor's words and wondered if she had heard him wrong: "I thought maybe I had been mistaken—because the right eye is good." When she got home, she called. Apparently, Dr. Berke thought it best to operate on the muscle below the right eye because the procedure was easier, involving fewer muscles, and had a greater chance of success. On the telephone, he admitted that it was very difficult to explain why surgeons operate on the good eye except over the years they have found out "it works out better."

~ ~ ~

My parents had some trouble arranging a time for the surgery. At first it was slated for March 15, but that had to be moved to April 21. When the morning at last arrived, they were rushing to get ready, and welcomed the distracting hubbub: "we were hurrying around so we didn't have time to think about it a lot." They were looking forward to getting the surgery over and, now that it was about to happen, "were quite calm about it." Dr. Berke had assured my mother that it would not be "any more serious than a tonsillectomy." But just as they were leaving, the surgeon's office called with news that the operation had to be postponed for a week because "there weren't any beds available in the nursery."

My mother took this news hard, becoming detached and self-absorbed. Friends from Idaho were scheduled to visit at the end of the week, but she decided that she would not prepare for their visit. "My house may be dirty because I've decided not to houseclean at this time." She said that she would try to be a good host, and show her friends a "nice time," but that she expected the visitors to "overlook the little things that are not done." She escaped to her back porch. "I want to get my rest and be outdoors as much as possible because I want to feel good at this time," and then, in a weary parenthesis, adds: "I was so happy to know it would be over soon." I run my thumb over these words, registering the depth of disappointment, here, this new low. She admitted that she was being childish: "Maybe I still have hopes—I'll grow up some time (ha)." Her solace was to watch Ron play in the sunlight. "Must close and get outside with Ronnie," she writes, "it is a gorgeous day." She was clearly fragile and felt the need to maintain some control over the gloom that was spreading through her, her sons playing on the lawn serving as a soothing anodyne. "I'm going to take care of myself and remain calm. I will admit it is hard with the delay, but will try to stay outdoors a lot with the boys."

~ ~ ~

"Organized crime does operate on a syndicated basis across state lines in the United States," Estes Kefauver says, his soft Tennessee accent turned brittle and tinny by the speakers of our family's *Sylvania* and his face a filmy, grainy shadow on the rounded screen. "That is a bigger, more sinister, and larger operation than we had ever suspected." My mother looks on, her legs pulled up on the sofa beside her as she liked to do, while racketeers and Mafia bosses are called before the committee: Willie Moretti, Joe Adonis, and Frank Costello. She watches Louis Fratto, the Midwest Mafia boss and brother of hit man Frankie "one-ear" Fratto, refuse to identify thugs in the Kansas City crime scene. Ironically, the coverage of the mob brings news from back home, but it is frustrating to watch. Even Kefauver cannot pry the secrets out of the mobsters.

When she gets tired of watching the black and white image of "Cockeyed Louie," my mother turns down the sound on the TV, and in silence pulls a volume of *The Book of Knowledge* from the shelf and opens to a section with a marker in it. It is on such a night that she reads the eight-page illustrated article about "eyes." I have no way of proving it, but I know for certain that she does because this section with its scientific terminology and detailed diagrams is her torment and her solace and her companion on lonely nights. It is her fetish.

"Eyes do not stay still," *The Book* explains. "They are constantly moving," following objects, looking from place to place. That innocuous comment is followed by two sentences that probably haunted her: *Our eyes and the eyes of other mammals move together. Both of them are always directed toward the thing they wish to see.* She has no choice but to read these words, though they add a fresh load of misery to her depression. Under the glow of the cathode ray tube, the chrysalis of her obsession forms around her. Her spirit flops away on wide wings while her eyes stare off, and her melancholic self burrows deep inside the segmented husk of her nightmare.

And I cannot join her there. I can look at the same photographs—touch pages that are identical to hers and close my eyes trying to picture her—but the shell of the glossy page protects the image and hides her. She wanted no one to follow her. I imagine the look on her face, when the eyes glaze blotting out the world of others and the gaze turns inward entranced by some ache there because I have seen that look in photos, and I'm sure that I saw her looking off that way when I was a boy, but I have never felt that kind of hopelessness in my life and am protected from it somehow. It was her secret and, like Cockeyed Louie Fratto, she ain't sayin' nothin'. We share much I know, looking once again out at the illustration of the six muscles of the eye which run between the eyeball and the bony wall that encases it, but I cannot reproduce in myself the feeling of dread that this page produced in her. I'm held back by a surface as smooth and hard as a bullet.

~ ~ ~

While writing the section on Ron's eyes, I dream of Dr. Jackman, my parents' marriage counselor from Dodge City, and at first I am not sure why. In my dream he sits on a sofa beside a tall wooden file cabinet and wears a three-piece flannel suit like the one my grandfather used to wear, with a fob watch and rimless glasses, and he fiddles in a fussy way with the seam of his slacks.

I pick up a bottle of bourbon as if it were a telephone receiver to talk to him. When I ask my Wonder Question, he sits back and places his hand on my mother's file which had been destroyed years ago but is available for him in heaven.

"That's confidential," he says in a clipped voice, smiling enigmatically.

Beside him on the sofa sits my mother wearing a suit with a blue pencil skirt. She holds her legs slanted demurely off to one side. I notice a faint smell of percolated coffee in the room.

"Read your book, Stevie," my mother says looking directly at me. I hear her slip rustle as she leans forward, holding out a volume of *The Book of Knowledge*.

"Your book."

~ ~ ~

At first, the eye operation looked like a success. Here is part of my mother's letter from May 4, 1954, which captures the feeling of the event.

"We arrived at the Institute at 9:30 and they took us to the nursery. It was very nice. Little glassed in bedrooms (about 10) and then a big playroom. The nurse was very nice and I undressed Ronnie—he was quiet and good. We walked into the playroom and two little toddlers came out to meet Ronnie. The nurse said it would be very nice of us to go shopping and come back at 2:00. She said Dr. Berke would operate on Ronnie at 1:00. So we drove downtown and shopped around. When we got back Ronnie was resting comfortably but still out. She said we should go home and call that evening and they usually remain pretty well out for that day and the next. We called that night and they said Ronnie had wakened and was hungry and that they had given him a bottle of water—and that we could visit him Friday between 2 – 3 o'clock. Max felt he should work—so I asked Jeanne to go visit with me and she was thrilled. Mary took care of Steve.

"That was quite a heart tugging experience. When I walked in he was resting on his tummy.

93

I said 'Ronnie—its Mommie.' He whispered Mommie and got to his feet groping for me (because both eyes were bandaged) and I picked him up. He was very dopey and didn't talk but just clung to me. Now and then he would say Mommie, Daddie, Jeannie or Steve while we were talking to him. I was beginning to wonder what to do about leaving when he suddenly mentioned ball. He loves balls. So Jeannie and the nurse found a ball for him. We put it in his hands and he said Ball—Ball—Ball. The nurse walked in and I handed Ronnie to her. She said 'I didn't know you liked balls Ronnie—we'll have to play catch.' I said 'Bye Ronnie we come back for you tomorrow. He whimpered a little but the nurse kept talking to him about the ball."

~ ~ ~

"It's like shooting into darkness," Dr. Berke had said when my mother asked about the chances of success in the operation.

Unfortunately, he missed. The optimists, my father and Dr. Berke, both said the eyes were working together though to be fair, Dr. Berke admitted that they were too swollen to be certain, and he had warned my parents that more operations might be necessary in the future. According to my mother's letter, my dad kept saying 'they're working together' over and over as if trying to talk himself, and my mother, into believing it. He was that way. It was my mother, the pessimistic realist, who could not bring herself to say that the eyes were working properly. She wrote that Ron watched TV with greater concentration which she took as a good sign, but she "couldn't be sure" that the eyes were fixed. She was right.

The eyes were not coordinated, a fact that became clear when the swelling went down.

The patch went back on sometime in September of 1954. Ron had gone without the patch all summer, but my mother knew that the problem had not been corrected and made an appointment with the ophthalmologist. Ron was sleepy at the time of the appointment so that the doctor saw the eyes "at their worst for the first time." He noticed that the left eye tended to roll up and that the right one dipped down a bit, and that the eyes were "not only crossed horizontally but vertically" which concerned him. Vertical control presents a greater challenge because "it involves twice as many muscles." The doctor was most alarmed though about possible vision loss and insisted that the patch be worn consistently. My mother admitted that she "was not shocked" by this news because she saw Ron every day and knew that problems had persisted. Still she regretted that she and Ron were in for a "long process," beginning with monthly visits to the doctor in order to take a sequence of measurements, and even though she had been warned early about the possibility of future operations, she admitted that she did not have the "calm dispositions" that others had.

There are almost no pictures of Ron during this time. My mother claimed that the camera was on the fritz—one time the flash bulb popped and caught fire, she mentioned, melding itself to the flash attachment when she snapped the shutter. But she did manage to get a Christmas photo of Ron and one of me reading books in front of the shelf that housed the encyclopedias and *The Books of Knowledge*. We are in matching footed pajamas and both of us have our hair combed and parted. I apparently got a kick out of my brother, and I am looking at him with a big smile on my face. He looks fixedly toward the camera with the beginning of a smile on his lips, a front baby tooth missing. The eyes are clearly visible, and, unless you are looking carefully, they appear fine, but when I examine the photo closely under a glass I see that the left eye drifts up a bit and the right one does slide slightly inward.

It was not until April 1955 that my brother's eyes were finally fixed. "We're very pleased with Ronnie's operation—they are very good," my mother wrote in a brief Easter note. "The doctor said Thurs. that they are synchronized and at the moment that is the most important thing." Still over the course of two-and-a half-years my brother had two eye operations and wore a patch on one eye nearly every day, a seesaw of successes and setbacks that took a toll on my mother.

~ ~ ~

I have a second dream of Dr. Jackman in heaven. I have three of these in fact, and they come in rapid succession during one night and between each dream I wake up briefly. I take notes right away trying to remember the swirl of images and words, but my dreams are slippery, resisting the coherence of sentences, and I can only approximate them as I write.

In my second dream, the doctor wipes his glasses with a small piece of lens paper as we talk, and when he puts the glasses on, his eyes are lost in the glare.

I pick up the bourbon bottle like a telephone receiver and ask my question though I cannot remember what it is.

"That's confidential as well," the doctor says firmly.

My mother sits beside him again, this time wearing a black slip and bra, with a white scarf, and a black purse. The slip falls in loose folds against her thin body.

When I repeat my question, speaking to her this time, she drapes an arm over Dr. Jackman's shoulder, bare white skin against his worsted suit. There is a faint smell of coconut in my dream.

"Play with your toys, Stevie," she says, lifting a balsa *Jetfire* in her fingertips and holding it out to me.

~ ~ ~

Wonder Question: What is the blind spot?

"There is a blind spot in both your eyes," *The Book of Knowledge* explains, a pucker of cells on the retina that lacks rods and cones and has no sensation of vision. The image that passes over this spot in the eye doesn't fade away or get smaller, but, rendered insubstantial as a dream, it just disappears—poof!—blending into the background. The surprise for me is that we do not find a dot in everything we see since the blind spot cannot register light, but the brain compensates for the lack of vision, painting it in with a neutral background. That is what the brain does, filling in the empty places of our memories and dreams for us, airbrushing away our flaws.

It can't help itself.

I look down at the page in *The Book of Knowledge* with the diagram for locating the blind spot. "There is always a little error in our sight," *The Book* says, sagely. So what am I missing in this story of my mother? What bullet hole has my mental airbrush nebulized away? What is the blind spot in my story?

~ ~ ~

It may be my grandfather. The apprehension that my mother experienced on the night of my grandfather's stroke, this shadowy link of sympathy between them, had a more sinister source, she believed, an insidious family curse hidden like a neutralizing blind spot in her story. Nowhere in my grandmother's correspondence does this topic appear, but, before she died, my grandmother confided in Barbara, telling her another family secret that had been kept from me by everyone, including my father.

According to my grandmother, my mother believed that she had contracted congenital syphilis, the disease having been passed to her in childbirth. Her depression brought on paranoid nightmares in which she imagined a million axial filaments, slimy microscopic fins, winding their way through her body, migrating along her central nervous system, contaminating her brain, and coming out in the eyes of her son. The depression that led to this nightmarish vision did not begin with my father and her marriage. It wound its way back to her father, my grandfather, the small-town doctor to whom she was devoted, the melancholy and withdrawn soul mate who was, she believed, the likely source of their fatal disease.

Given the strong emotional bond between my mother and grandfather, this dark untruth was probably absorbed like a blow to the body. It is possible that my grandfather did have syphilis. My father told Barbara that if he did he probably contracted it as a doctor while delivering a baby, but my grandmother insisted that *she* did not have syphilis and that my mother's belief that she had contracted it at birth was "crazy." Still, my mother thought it was true and also believed that Ron's eye problems were the result of the disease being passed down to him in childbirth. These paranoid notions, growing out of an unfounded sense of contagion within the family, compounded the pain of her "year of blackness" in 1953.

The stroke that my grandfather suffered two years later was light: the mild paralysis on one side of his body largely went away over the course of the next year. By April, he was able to rake leaves using both hands. But his vision continued to remain so blurry that he was unable to drive a car, a detail of his illness that would not have escaped my mother.

~ ~ ~

What was it like to be in my mother's mind then as she sat outside all morning, day after day, smoking cigarettes and watching us play in the yard, fending off the dreariness that she cannot scrub, wash, or sweep away while a wicker basket on a countertop somewhere in the house behind her piled high with dirty laundry?

The yard of patchy green descended to an opening in the woods, the threshold of a dark corridor into the trees where I liked to rummage for fossils. I poked through the stone pile hunting for the calcified gooey remains of exoskeletons cast in stone whose pictures I had found in *The Book of Knowledge*: three-lobed trilobites, coiled ammonites, and armored chitons. Is that what she saw, me poking through the arthropodal rubble at the woods' edge filling my pockets with rocks?

Maybe she watched Ron in his striped tee shirt playing in the sun with a ball like the one that Jeannie and the nurse found for him at the hospital when the first operation on Ron's eyes left him blindfolded. "He loves balls," she said then. So, maybe.

It was a "gorgeous day," in late April, she wrote, "sunny and warm with a nice breeze." Did she close her eyes? Just to rest them and stop the thoughts, the sun rising higher and higher, brightening the morning, as her shadow and our shadows shrank and turned blacker, and seemed to recoil into our bodies.

Andrew Solomon calls depression "The Noonday Demon" and William Styron describes it as "darkness visible," Milton's words for Satan in *Paradise Lost*. My mother called it "our year of blackness" that even the morning sun could not dispel which is one reason why early mornings were the hard time.

Maybe she looked into the gorgeous day with its steady beam of sun, as the lawn flowed down and away, her mind clinging to the idyll of children at play on the green or along the woods' edge, the Celtic threshold of childlike wonder, but could not in her gloom sustain the illusion. When she set her pen down beside the ashtray and gazed at her children, the shadows of her own fears dulled the sun. "Gorgeous" was never the right word, and "thresholds" invite familiar foes. Maybe she looked down the barrel of the darkened corridor under the canopy of trees and flicked an ash, oblivious to the curlicues of smoke that formed beside her hair, while a grisly space opened in her mind, a patrimonial pit littered with paranoid delusions of spirochetes eating into our brains.

~ ~ ~

Dr. Jackman sits on a sofa and has taken off his suit jacket and vest. It is July in Kansas, after all. He wears a loose-fitting, long-sleeved white shirt with a stiff collar, a pair of suspenders, and a short red tie. His jacket hangs on a rack. I pick up the bottle of bourbon and hold it to my ear. I know his conversations are confidential, but I ask my wonder question anyway.

As I ask it, I realize that Dr. Jackman is my grandfather.

My mother lies completely naked with her head in his lap, facing up. Her white skin glows slightly and her breasts are girlish, standing up in small mounds. Her hair is in slight disarray as if a ribbon had been pulled from it and her black slip lies crumpled on the floor.

I notice a faint smell of buttered toast in the room.

When I ask my question, she says nothing.

Her eyes are closed.

I wake up, feverish.
Incest?

~ ~ ~

Wonder Questions: What happens when ink dries?

So this is it—to write my *Book of Pillage and Plunder* I have turned over boxes, upended bookshelves and ripped open letters until I unearthed evidence of disease and suspicions of incest in my family. The year of blackness is a trail of ink that I followed to this black well. And now Waconda Spring is so murky that I can't see into it at all.

My grandmother told my mother that she noticed a change in her handwriting during 1953 when my mother was depressed. It is true that the handwriting in earlier letters was often more open and spontaneous, and the lettering in 1953 is more precise and carefully done, prettier, I guess, but the differences are not obvious or consistent and I certainly would not have noticed if my grandmother had not mentioned it.

What I *do* see in all of the letters is that the ink from my mother's hand stains the page leaving blind spots that I fill with my own speculations, dreams, and nightmares. In the end I am no different than my grandmother, seeking redemption by scouring the curlicues of Mother's words for clues, a bogus graphologist pausing over a sinewy tail on a capital D, a cramped "e" at the end of my name, or a hastily drawn ampersand as if these strokes will conjure up a precise psychogram of my mother's emotional state.

In the end it is only ink.

"When ink dries," *The Book of Knowledge* explains, "the watery part has evaporated into the air, while the solids remain in, and on, the paper." My mother sits at the table writing her letters, laying down the solids that I am reading now, the remains of words "in and on" the page, while the truth about her floats off of the paper and evaporates like a diaphanous curl of breath in cold air.

~ ~ ~

In 1928 Dr. Lloyd B. Dickey argued in the *Journal of the American Medical Association*, that "strabismus"— another medical term for crossed eyes—was "well known as a presenting complaint, or symptom" of syphilis, although he ruled out congenital syphilis as a cause. He argued that the connection between crossed eyes and the venereal disease had been long known informally by doctors at least back to 1902. Maybe my mother's fears were not just paranoia. Syphilis can damage the eyes in many ways, and doctors at the time apparently believed the connection between the disease and crossed eyes was strong. Perhaps my mother's fears were based on evidence from the medicine of her time. Perhaps my grandmother was a latent carrier of the illness.

"Craziness or a cry for help," I wrote, scribbling notes when I woke from my third version of the dream, the word "incest" on my lips. What *was* the special relationship between my mother and my grandfather? Was it a secret too awful to admit?

"My mother was a nurse-trainee," I explained to Barbara while she was getting dressed for work not long after I had my dreams. "As a science major in college, she would have known *something* about syphilis. Maybe it was not paranoia on her part at all, but a legitimate possibility. Maybe she knew something that she couldn't tell, certainly not to her mother. Maybe she could only hint at the true problem." And maybe, I thought without saying, the clues have been delivered to me as a confession of the unspeakable. My mother believed that she could sense my grandfather's stroke even though he was half a continent away. Maybe she was longing for someone in the future, some me, to sense her pain. I have to admit, I was starting to get a little crazy myself.

Barbara assured me first that incest was highly unlikely. "Your grandmother said that your mother was *convinced* that she had contracted syphilis from *her.*" That conviction is borne out in the letters because much of my mother's anxiety had to do with Ron's eye problem being congenital. And on the other matter, that my mother had syphilis? Barbara adjusted her blouse and quoted my grandmother: "She said that it was 'crazy because *she* never had syphilis.'" Nor did I, I would add as I thought about it later, or my brother or my father.

The disease my mother and my grandfather shared was depression. That was the pain that lashed them to a mutual woe despite the miles separating them. It produced the paranoid fears of other diseases, a common side effect of depression, and it was enough to kill them both.

~ ~ ~

What is the source of these dream messages we can't face by day? These ancestral visitations embedded in our genetic code, shaped by forgotten memories and backlit by our unspoken fears—how far back do they go? They are far stranger than our words can capture and feel preverbal. Images in my dreams seem to float and fall and morph seamlessly into new images so that making distinctions—the white spaces between words and thought—distorts them. They have no blind spots.

Do I recapitulate the night thoughts of horses and fish and amoebae in my dreams? Did the Paleozoic mental activity of the fossilized trilobite in my fingertips as a boy illuminate some chamber of my reptile brain?

The Book of Knowledge is not much help. "Many modern psychologists believe that, if we could understand

103

our dreams, they could tell us much about our feelings and attitudes toward life," it says with little enthusiasm. It points out that dreams often exaggerate experiences and make what happens more exciting than life, suggesting that these phantoms of the night mind cannot be trusted to deliver truth. In the end it dismisses them claiming that "many people think that our dreams don't mean anything at all." Dreams are not *The Book's* way of knowing, I suppose.

In the final months of my grandmother's life she suffered from dementia and could not distinguish between her dream and her waking states. Occasionally the dreams were pleasant, even funny, causing her to laugh inexplicably. While we visited her in the nursing home she heard the toilet running and turned to us. "Listen to that," she said, in her hospital bed, "the Solomon River." Most of the time she was terrified, day or night, by the monsters that attacked her. I'm not demented yet, but when I wake up in the night it takes a long time to shake the dream that has been playing itself out under my closed eyelids.

So these dreams—and this is my question—these three parallel dreams about my mother and Dr. Jackman that came to me in rapid succession, are they a message from her? A message in the bottle of bourbon I hold to my ear. And if they are, what is she saying through these nightmarish phantoms that hang upside down like bats in the back of my brain by day and, at night, flutter awake in a flurry of wings just under my eyelids?

"Your toys," she said. "Your book."

Play. Read.

And then she closed her eyes.

~   ~   ~

Wonder Question: How can we see with our eyes shut?

Our eyelids never block out all of the light. According to *The Book of Knowledge*, when "you shut your eyes tight and turn your head toward a dark corner of the room, and then toward a near-by lamp you will discover that you can, even with your eyes shut, tell the difference between darkness and bright light."

Seeing never stops.

If you look at something bright—a window, a television screen, a shock of blond hair in sunlight—and close your eyes, very strange things can happen, because the image refuses to go away. "Sometimes the after-image is bright," *The Book* explains, before adding ominously that it is also "sometimes dark."

There is only one way to completely get rid of what we see, and eventually my mother did that, but even then, who knows?

~ ~ ~

By late 1954 my mother's year of blackness, which dragged on really for almost two years, was over. Her depression was not defeated, but held in check. She underwent a "D. and C." procedure—dilation and curettage—for reasons that are not clear. It may have involved problems with her menstruation or complications from Ron's birth. It may also have been an abortion. But afterwards she claimed that it improved her outlook on life. She admitted that she was a "little blue" before the procedure, as if the "upsetting" feelings of 1953 were coming back, but after the procedure she immediately felt better. "I had the D. and C. on Monday and came out of the hospital Thursday night feeling absolutely wonderful with no worries and all that rest." Cryptically, she added this: "shock and worry had made me sick and the shock and worry connected with the D. and C. had snapped me back again."

Feeling better allowed her to discuss her problems more frankly, and she uses the word "depressed" for the first time in her letters. "Now I can't see why I was so depressed," she writes dismissively, "because I have every confidence that Ronnie's eyes will be straightened soon and things will be back to normal." She may have had a small relapse into depression sometime after Christmas in 1954, but by April 1955, when the last surgery on my brother's eyes was finished, she seemed baffled by her mental illness and writes about it abstractly as if she didn't recognize herself. "I don't know why this thing affected me so deeply because before this I never thought I was the emotional type."

She never defeated the disease that returned periodically in less virulent form after 1953 and ultimately roared back in 1961 and destroyed her, but she did manage it by stealing joy where she could. She loved children and the whole idea of childhood, and when it didn't turn dark and shadowy the Celtic threshold of innocent wonder brought her joy. Her favorite musical was *Peter Pan*, that tale of perpetual childhood about a character whose shadow keeps falling off. My mother loved the spontaneity of children, enjoyed their impishness, and admired their honesty. When my grandmother mentioned an irritating feud that Ron as a child had with one of his friends, my mother used the incident to stand up for kids in general. "Yes, I remember the rivalry between Ronnie & Doug," she wrote. "That is what makes children delightful—they show every emotion. As we get older we cover them up until we never know how other people feel, or even ourselves sometimes."

Both my dad and my mother had been raised as only children, and my mother delighted in having the enlarged family dynamics created by more than one child. She admitted, after Ron was born, that she had little time for sleep and groused like all mothers that the schedule was hectic. Even with a half-hour nap in the afternoon she found herself exhausted by the time dinner was done, but the pace and commotion of family brought her pleasure. "I'm still quite tired by the time I finish the dishes," she explained, "but I really enjoy having the two children—it already seems more like a family."

She loved her Ronnie. Always struggling to gain weight herself she marveled in his good appetite and chubby body. "Ronnie is cute as a bug," she mentioned, in the same letter in which she admitted the gloomy news that she had not been honest with her parents because she was hiding the problem with Ron's eyes. The squint did not dull her enthusiasm for her boy. "He is still a good looking baby—and quite large—his little body is so round and firm not flabby." Her joy was tempered by concern about the upcoming surgeries. "I became very upset," she conceded, but her delight is unmistakable as well.

Once when I was playing a toy clarinet, Ron grabbed it from me. When I complained to my father, he said, "you can take care of it. Its your fight." So I punched Ron. For a while we exchanged blows and Ron "came running" to his mother "crying." "You started this Ronnie," she said and refused to pick him up. So Ron marched back over to me and we exchanged blows again. This pattern of fighting followed by Ron crying and retreating to his mother went on three more times until I grabbed him while he took a swing and we both rolled on the floor laughing. "Never a dull moment," my mother wrote.

Ron would throw himself into the center of any situation, especially if he did not belong, and my mother enjoyed watching the little showman. Once, when I was five and he two, I had a girlfriend named Jessica over to play, and Ron was "quite taken with her," too, so he performed for her doing the usual antics. When she and I sat on the floor to watch TV, Ron "plopped down beside Jessica and looked up at her with wonder in his eyes." Eventually Mom sequestered Ron by setting up a fence, keeping him on her side so that he could not pester Jessica and me, while she wrote a letter. When she got to the part of the letter describing how good Ron was about not breaking things and learning to put "no, no's" back carefully when told to, she had to stop and take the words back. "Wouldn't you know—just as I was writing this" Ron broke through the barrier and "banged Jessica on the head with a rubber plane." Mom seemed to take it all in stride: "you know boys," she wrote, "and Ronnie is a true boy."

The story about Ron and Jessica and me is in the same letter in which my mother talked about the Machiavellian intrigues at Lederle, the "apple-polishing" and "rushing" of bosses' wives. It is also the letter in which she wrote that "our year of blackness" was behind us, and even though there would be blackness ahead, Ron's impishness showed her a different way. "Ron gets away with murder," my father once told my mother, and it is true she often went "soft" with him, but that softness was her better nature which Ron seemed to touch directly.

"He is a little character, but so much fun," Mom wrote at Easter when Ron was two. My mother had made baskets for us and she and Dad had hidden small nests of eggs in the living room. I apparently showed up "my eyes full of wonder" because the Easter Bunny "had been there," but I was wrong. It was not the Easter Bunny I had heard. "So we got up to see," my mother wrote, "and there was Ronnie, his mouth and both hands full of candy." My mother loved it. "He is at a delightful stage

now. He is saying many words and—throwing kisses—
and everything." This is from the letter in which my
mother discovered that the operation was delayed and she
was too ill to do housework or prepare for guests.
Instead, she preferred to watch us play in the yard at the
edge of the woods—"that is relaxing," she explained.

One incident from our childhood—the time that
Ron tried to fly—is legendary in our family. It happened
in January of 1956, about the time of my grandfather's
stroke, another difficult time for her. Ron and I still talk
about it occasionally, although I don't think either of us
remembers it well. Here is my mother's version.

I'll have to tell you the trick Ronnie did
about two weeks before Christmas. It could
have been very serious, but we were lucky that
he was only hurt a very little. He had been and
still is quite intrigued with Superman. I kept
telling him it was only make believe but couldn't
seem to make him understand that people
couldn't fly. The boys would tie bath towels
around their necks and make believe they were
flying around the living room. One night at
dinnertime I was in the kitchen cooking. Max
was reading the paper on the divan. Ronnie
came up and had him tie on his bath towel
cloak. He proceeded over to the cellar steps and
took off. We heard him bump down the stairs
and both ran terrified to see what had happened.
We don't know from where he took off but we
were fortunate because he only had a bump on
his forehead and a scratched nose and mouth. It
all healed up in about three days. The crowning
blow was the next morning as I was giving them
breakfast I heard Steve say, "how was it flying."
Ronnie said, "It was fun for a little bit."

109

~ ~ ~

And what about me?

"We have a big time making the shadows on the wall," my mother wrote, and after reading the letter I remembered doing that with her and my dad though I have trouble picturing the scene. Did we turn off the TV and cook up some popcorn? Did we lift the shade off of the lamp for higher contrast? I picture the room washed out with a white light so maybe that is true, though this memory has clearly been airbrushed.

I did take away two vivid sets of images from the event, one about my dad and one about my mom. I remember making a shadow of a dog on the wall, causing it to open and close its mouth. My father did the same shadow except he was able to create a bright spot for the eye in the dog's head. Somehow he raised the knuckle of one finger just enough to pass light, and I thought it was amazing. Dad showed me the trick, and I gave it a try, but my fingers could not bow upward enough to make it work.

My mother's hands created the simplest, and most lovely, of shadow shapes: a bird in flight. Her fingers were long and slender, and when she formed her bird the wings flapped slowly, opening and closing on air, the outspread fingertips suggesting feathers. So I try it now, turning out all of the lights in my study except for one. Standing by a blank wall I cross my hands with the palms facing inward, locking my thumbs. When I lift the bundle of fingers and palms into the lamplight a bird shape floats onto the wall and by moving my thumbs I create the hungry beak clacking in air. My fingers are stubbier than Mom's, I know, but the shape of the bird elongating beyond my fingertips is largely the same as the one her hands cast in 1954.

110

My mother took joy in my eagerness to read by flashlight under my covers and pull down volumes of *The Book of Knowledge* and spread them on the floor. She was as excited as I was about my collections of fossils and dinosaurs and pennies, and shared my love of silent, beautiful satellites floating through space. Sometimes I forget that my mother gave me more than this handful of shadows that I carry around in my genetic predisposition to dreams and nightmares, but this little trick of wings on the wall reminds me that the debt for much of who I am now runs deep in my childhood. I raise my hands so that the shadow will ascend the wall, but when I lift them to eye level it is my own hands I see, not the shadows, with thumbs linked, though the shadow brought them to light for me, and the wonder is that they are *her* hands, alive now in mine.

"Have been raking some stones away," my mother wrote in the spring of 1951 when I was nearly two. "Also planted six pansies by the front porch." My mother never thought of herself as much of a gardener and was skeptical about the prospects for these six seedlings, especially in our neighborhood full of kids in Nanuet. "Between my hard luck with the flowers," she wrote, "and the children, chances are pretty slim." But she loved the Crayola colors and dancing gaiety of the flowers and simply could not resist: "pansies are so pretty I thought I would give them a try." Cultivated from an English viola tricolor named heartsease, each pansy wears a clown face: two black eyes and a smeared mouth against a gaudy colored ruff. The heads are nearly too big for the stems which bow and bob under the weight making them jiggle wildly and the leaves below open wide like the sleeves of a buffoon's frock.

The letters chronicle our many attempts to grow pansies, but I was unable to remember any of them until I read about our last attempt. We had moved from New York to Deerfield, Illinois by then and my mother, who was on the verge of her final depression, was preoccupied. My father was often gone, which caused her to be anxious and worried, and when he was at home they fought, so for a while she neglected our pansy project. "I hang my head in shame," she wrote, "when speaking of Steve's flower garden. He worked so diligently to get the small area ready and we were so busy we only planted a few plants."

"Pansies," I whispered, when I read the letter for the first time last year, setting it on my knee and looking out the bay window of our house in Georgia to my own small garden, "yes!" A small *frisson*. I could picture us. Mom and I were behind the garage in a little sunny plot of land, and it was hot. I was on my knees digging in the dirt while she, wearing clam diggers, sat down on her haunches separating the tangled roots and handing the plants to me one at a time. This was June—too late to plant from seed—so we were putting in seedlings with jiggling blooms. I remember her hands, the nails painted red and the fingers curled around the base of the plants. I took each one carefully from her fingers and set them in the dirt, a gentle transfer, the memory of it easing the heart as I sat back in my chair, and after she finished she wiped the dirt from her hands. When I got the last seedling in the ground, I sat up and she pointed to the eyes and mouth of one of the blossoms drawing the face with her painted fingernail for me, and I know that when she did I looked back at her and smiled with the sun in my eyes, so in this distant memory the scene suddenly blanches white, and as usual with these memories of my mother I can't make out her face.

All I see is the glare.

~ ~ ~

Wonder Question: Were all flowers once wild?

"Certainly all flowers once were wild—and all animals, too," *The Book of Knowledge* answers, but the wonder question is really an excuse to talk about the way horticulturists have cross-bred, hybridized, and grafted wild flowers so that their domesticated versions are extravagant but delicate variations of the hardy originals. The five petal nasturtium was long a popular garden flower in Europe and the United States, but to double the number of petals, Joseph Simson, the president of the Burpee Seed Company had over 40,000 crosses made. To accelerate the process of mutation Burpee created large, heated greenhouses at home and sent seeds to climates that were warm year-round.

"One evening," *The Book of Knowledge* explains, "Mr. Burpee was walking through the greenhouses looking at his new double nasturtiums when all at once he noticed one that was different from all the rest." It did not have the ten or even twelve petals of the double nasturtium, but "about fifty petals and looked like a begonia." He dubbed this lucky accident the "super-double nasturtium" and was eventually able to cultivate super doubles for sale. *The Book of Knowledge* is quick to point out that these new creations are precarious and require attentive nurturing to flourish. Elaborate orchids, double roses, super-double nasturtiums, and other hybrid flowers can over time revert to the wild, and without proper care "our gardens will return sometimes more or less completely to their natural state." In the end it is not easy to cultivate Pan out of the pansy.

~ ~ ~

But my mother certainly tried. As a girl, she participated in a dancing and gymnastic program that required her to twist herself into impossible positions and remain still. One of her suits for these contests was a one-piece combination of a leather vest and puffy, short, acrobatic pants worn over a white blouse. The picture was taken in my grandparents' back yard—I recognize the characteristic round stones arranged around the trees from my own childhood vacations in Kansas—and in this garb she looks like the elfin Peter Pan, not the Mary Martin version, but perhaps the Eve Le Gallienne Pan in tights and vest from a popular version of the story which played at that time at the Civic Repertory Theater in New York.

My mother wrote about "the lessons and the struggles" that went into the training for her acrobatic and dance performances. These dance teams were very popular, apparently, and she performed throughout the state with her small company. It appears, based on the one photo I have of her doing a routine, as though her task was to assume difficult, but graceful, positions and hold them. In another picture she is again in the backyard, this time performing a pose on a towel in front of dark cottonwood trees. She wears a shiny, sequined outfit with a puffy elastic bottom that exposes her knobby knees and long thighs, and lies head down on the towel with her face turned toward us. Her arms extend outstretched on the ground behind her, and she has lifted her legs high in the air so that one is upright above her body and the other bent at the knee, the toe of her shoe resting improbably close to her head. She looks like a pretzel turned on its end.

The expression on her face is an attempt at a managed serenity, and I look at it under the magnifying glass. Her mouth is a straight line, a stoic half smile, and her cheeks and forehead look relaxed as if she has learned to attain some level of repose even while maintaining this contorted position, but her eyes are closed and there is a tightening around them that suggests pain, and the eyebrows raised high and arched are also clues that the impossible hurts. I set down the magnifying glass and hold the picture at arm's length to take it all in, and understand that my mother's life often felt to her like this pose, an unnatural contortion of the self held in place by will until the quiver at the eyes, the tightened smile, the terrified glance, give it away. The face jammed down on the towel bears the facial expression she wore for many of her pictures as she sat erect for photos on the couch wearing make-up to hide her dark eyes. It is the face she wore for my father between their shouting matches. It is the creamy emptiness between the lines of her letters. It is the androgynous Peter with all of the Pan twisted out of her. It is the face in her coffin.

~ ~ ~

Both Peter Pan and the pansy take their names from the satyr Pan, a Greek God depicted in the art and literature of antiquity as an ugly man with horns in his brow and the legs of a goat, a pagan spirit that has little to do with the most famous British version of the deity, *Peter* Pan, the creation of James Matthew Barrie. The Greek Pan looks old and degenerate, more of a Captain Hook than a Peter, but the bronze statue of Peter Pan, erected by Barrie in Kensington Gardens in honor of his creation, is all innocence. Leaning back with one arm in the air and his head bent forward, this version of the child of the woods blows an elegantly curved, single reed pipe. He is Pan reduced to pansy, the Edwardian Pan, stripped of the base passions of his Greek model, a representation of the freedom of childhood rather than the embodiment of natural urges. He wears a leather tunic that comes, discreetly, just over the thighs and is more impish than erotic, the boy who refuses to grow up and would, Barrie explains, trade "a kiss for a thimble."

It was a trade my mother longed for. She kept her demons at bay by domesticating them, and though the mix was precarious and temporary and the furies that would not be contained for long exploded like seedpods within her in the end, the version of herself and of her children folded into each other on the family sofa and framed by the comfortable glow of black and white TV, gave them all a measure of peace and happiness. Sanitized balm.

~ ~ ~

"We are looking forward to Monday night on T.V." my mother wrote in 1956. We still lived in Nanuet, but the year of blackness was behind us, the shadows apparently dispelled for now, and the letters are newsy and come more frequently. "The play Peter Pan will be given again with Mary Martin playing the part." Watching the show had become an annual ritual for our family. "We saw it last year and the boys were completely awed by it." My mother thought Mary Martin was "marvelous" and deserved her "rave reviews" because she had "a charm that makes anyone who watches her feel like it's a big, bright, wonderful world." I am sure, as I think back to those television performances, that I create a compound ghost of them in my mind. Mom and Dad sit on the sofa, though in the 1956 viewing my mother mentions that Dad had to work late to prepare a speech and was not there. My brother and I are in our pajamas lying on the carpet with our faces propped up on our arms watching the show. There is popcorn set out on a TV tray, a ubiquitous piece of furniture in the 50's, and we have sodas in bottles. These are special nights so we get to stay up. Later, as we get tired, we join Mom on the sofa leaning this way and that to stay awake.

I have trouble remembering the opening scene of the musical—the set up with the dog being sent out of the nursery and Peter's shadow being tucked in a drawer—but I do remember the glitter of Tinker Bell on the drawn window shutters in the dark, flitting about to the sound of chimes after the children go to sleep. As the music grows eerie, the window opens wide on a backdrop of the night sky filled with stars and in glides Peter arms outstretched and smiling wearing tights and a shirt with a leafy fringe. He has come to retrieve his shadow which Mrs. Darling, the mother of the children, snatched from him and hid in a drawer. When Peter floats through the window, the wonders begin.

For me, Peter Pan is forever that figure hovering among the stars at the nursery window, a dangle of moving parts suspended in air by a hidden wire. The androgynous boy, part woman and part marionette, who can fly in search of his shadow and find it. The pre-adolescent boy at the top of the stairs surveying the world of broken glass and smeared mascara from a safe distance. This opening scene may stay in my mind because it is mirrored at the end of the play which I watched again recently in YouTube clips. Wendy and the children have returned home without Peter and we sense that time has passed. Once again the nursery is dark and we wait with anticipation. My mother wrote that by the time we watched the show in 1956 I knew what would happen next but my brother did not. She said that the show was thrilling, and I "enjoyed it very much," but that "it was really Ronnie's time." Of course, at the end of the show Peter returns to take Wendy's daughter, Jane, instead of Wendy, but Ron could not foresee that. He was worried that once the Darling children had returned home from Never Land that he wouldn't see Peter Pan again and was disappointed, but, as he watched, the shutters to their nursery opened, the stars glittered in a nighttime sky and Peter came flying through the window again. Ron "threw his arms into the air" and, to my mother's delight, shouted. "There he is!"

~ ~ ~

118

But the character of Peter Pan, who was born when James Barrie's brother died as a boy, is not entirely innocent. David was the chosen son whose intelligence created high expectations in the family. When he was thirteen, he was sent to live with his older brother Alexander in Edinburgh in the hope that he might earn a scholarship to the university. His mother was reluctant to let him go, and, as Bruce K. Hanson writes in *The Peter Pan Chronicles*, "she was stunned for life when David was fatally injured in a skating accident." According to Barrie's memoir, she would wander the house asking "Is that you?" into the dark rooms believing in her grief that David had returned, and James had to answer that it was only he, not David, whom she had heard. For a while he tried to imitate David's voice to please his mother, an agonizing ventriloquism for a young boy who has lost his older brother, but it did not help. "Margaret Ogilvy would spend the rest of her life mourning David," writes Hanson. "Jamie would grow older and David would always remain a boy."

The boy from 'Never Never Never Land.'

~   ~   ~

It is a cryptic phrase, rendered opaque by its variations. In the earliest productions, J. M. Barrie identified the land of The Lost Boys as "Never Never Never Land." Later it was reduced to "Never Never Land" and in the Mary Martin production it became simply "Never Land." But if you replace the word "land" with "life" the true meaning of Peter's adopted home is clear. "Never Life" is a land for children, like Peter, who died on the day they were born. In this distant place, the Pirate Kingdom of Lost Boys is a corner of the graveyard set apart for a stillborn life that never quite happened except in the wishes and dreams of his mother, and the music here is the distant grief-drenched melody of a mother's last lullaby to an empty crib.

"Never Never Life" introduces a new twist, the double negative, by a stroke of logic, turning death into an impossibility. It is the land of eternal life where never-life never happens, and Peter, who rules over this island of eternal childhood, will forever be a boy as Wendy and the rest of the world grow old and die. It is Mrs. Barrie's David, and David is all that Jamie Barrie could never never not be. While Peter inhabits this will o' the wisp, he lives an un-unlife of constant adventure, a Romantic sublime no longer hemmed in by Edwardian proprieties or expectations. He is free because he is freed from the adult responsibilities that attend love and death.

"Never Never Never Life" is a different matter altogether, the nullifications piling up and confounding logic. Some might puzzle the phrase out logically to arrive at the bad news, but most just feel it in the gut. By adding another negation, Barrie draws three black lines under the word "never," magnifying the loss, and the cumulative effect of the italics is a darkening of life. It is not just a land for those babies who have lost their lives, it is a nightmare terrain where the principle of life itself has been snuffed out, a gloomy Erebus without affection, fruitfulness, or nurture—mere existence drained of the milk of human kindness.

Never Never Never Land is life without mother.

~ ~ ~

"In the past when you looked at pictures of your mother's photographs you always saw a shadow in them," Barbara said on that morning early on in the writing of this book, and in many ways I am saddened that I must use such a conventional trope for evil, but this shadow is everywhere in my story, and only now am I beginning to understand what it means. I am not drawn to the shadow floating behind the image of my mother beside her toy airplane on a cold Kansas morning because the shadow is in the picture. Nor am I drawn to it, I realize now, simply because I know what will happen to her in advance which is what I used to believe. It is not some adumbration of a future she is unable to see, hanging behind her as a warning of what is to come.

No, the shadow is mine. It is her story still living in me, and she hides by clinging to me and never letting go. When I move my arm across the blank wall with the light behind me, the hand drags her shadow with it. When I go my own way making a life as a teacher and a father and a writer forgetting about her as was her wish for decades, I do not entirely shake her, any more than my quick hand can lose its shadow. When I flee, there she is at my heels, my flat, two-dimensional accomplice. And yet, when I try to see her, to find the drawer where Mrs. Darling, who is also my mother and my accomplice, has stuffed her, she disappears, or, more accurately blends into everything else, the way a shadow is subsumed in the greater darkness when the shade is put back on the lamp and the lamp extinguished. When I do find the drawer and lift her out she falls through my fingers, her olive complexion passed through me to my daughter leaving no trace of her behind in my pale, freckled skin.

I have none of her. I am drenched in her, and I have none of her.

Sometimes my mother returns to me in the oddest of places. I saw her in a drawing on the back of an envelope from the hand of my father and as a recumbent figure on Dr. Jackman's couch of my nightmares. She is the silhouette of wings in flight and the hands of the old man that cast the shadows on the wall. She is Margaret Ogilvy and David and Mrs. Darling and Peter Pan. She is the Edwardian Pan and the clown face on the pansy. She is my father and the opposite of my father. She is my grandmother's enemy and friend and confidante, my grandfather and his illness, and she is a windswept grave marked with rotting flowers on the prairie.

All of those versions of her cast a shadow of me.

~ ~ ~

In the musical Peter's mother does in a way return— at least in song. The song takes place in the cave where Peter Pan lives, an underground dwelling deep in the woods and far away from the pirate ship, the Jolly Roger. Above the cave is a setting of windswept trees against a dark blue background, while underground all is ocher and softly lit. To enter the cave, Peter ducks into the bowl of a hollow tree and slides down a fireman's pole without using his hands. The cave has one large chamber where he, the Lost Boys, Tiger Lily and the Indians smoke a peace pipe and dance, but it has hidden recesses backstage that open onto a fireplace, a kitchen, and the boys' bedrooms, little domestic cubby holes for The Lost Boys. Peter lives in the cave with Wendy who by this point in the play pretends to be the mother of the boys. They call Peter "Father," and he enjoys the pretense of sitting in an easy chair at night while the children bring him slippers, a pipe, and the newspaper.

Before the children go to bed, Wendy asks Peter to sing a "lullaby." At the word Peter jumps, startled, but when he repeats it his mood softens and he smiles. He looks off, a single oboe playing in the background, and speaking in a child's voice says that he does remember a lullaby. Hesitantly, at first, he starts to sing "Distant Melody." This cradle song begins like a fairy tale with "once upon a time" and the lyrics are a string of clichés, but it is the way the words are sung—so unlike other moments in the musical—that really matters. Most of the time when Mary Martin plays Peter, she pitches her voice high, creating the tinny, clear, and slightly annoying crow of an adolescent boy, but when she performs this lullaby, her singing falls into a more natural range, opening the lower registers of a woman's voice, and the song becomes the lullaby of a mother inside a lullaby sung by a boy. When I watch a clip from the movie on YouTube more than fifty years later, and hear the mother's song in the boy, I realize that the performance that my mother and I watched together is *our* story then *and* now.

In the lyrics, Peter hears his mother comforting him by singing to him, or singing, perhaps, to the empty crib, assuring the baby that he is never alone because of her love. At the ends of the lines, Mary Martin milks words such as "low" and "near" and "afraid" and "alone," words that convey the emotion and tell the story of the song. When her voice rises on the phrase "all is well" she smiles and holds the note on the word "well," as if she, in her role as mother, can by the assurance in her voice demonstrate that the sentiment is true. All pretense that Mary Martin is a boy simply washes away as the actress's face assumes a radiant expression of maternal love. This is not Peter who protects with stratagems and tricks and disguises; this is a mother who offers love alone as a last stand in a world marked by loss and death. When she reaches the penultimate line and her voice rises in a crescendo on the word "know," her eyebrows, penciled in by some make-up artist, rise in crescents toward her hairline, and her face looks hopeful, but when she rides the last line slowly down to the final phrase, "long ago," with her hands clasped anxiously in her lap, the chimes strike a falling scale of discordant notes bringing the lullaby within a lullaby to an end. The mother disappears leaving a lost boy in her place as well as an old man watching alone with his fingers on the screen.

~ ~ ~

My favorite photograph from my childhood was taken when the three of us—my brother, my mother, and me—were on the sofa in Nanuet watching TV. My dad snapped it around 1956, the last year that we saw Peter Pan together, and Ron and I are in identical pajamas that look like space suits with a diagonal stripe across the front and a round collar at the neck. Ron, who is four, has a dopey look on his face as if he has stayed up past his bedtime, but he is awake and watching the show. He sports a dark crew cut. My parents have allowed my hair to grow out a bit, so it is parted, and I wear a face filled with wide-eyed wonder as we watch the screen.

I have no idea what we are watching—it may or may not be Peter Pan—but the photo has the feel of those special nights. My mother looks completely relaxed and at ease in a way that is rare in her pictures. She leans back in the sofa with her left arm around Ron holding his hand in her fingers. Her legs, bent at the knees, are pulled up on cushions beside her, and I am nestled in the hollow they make, my elbow leaning on her hip while her right arm encloses me from behind and her hand cups my other elbow. She wears her jeans rolled up, exposing her calf, and has on white socks and scuffed saddle Oxfords.

She is thirty and at the height of her beauty. Her thick hair is pulled back from her face revealing high cheekbones, a long, thin nose, lips in a faint smile painted petal red, and dark, sultry eyes. The face is rounded and smooth, with no tension this time around the eyes. She wears a dark blouse with bright white buttons and sleeves rolled up to her elbows and looks healthy and athletic. What moves me about the scene is how relaxed and comfortable we all are, our bodies tumbling together in a way that seems natural and easy. Even the pillow at her feet—a large, brown, shapeless thing with piping running along its seams—adds to the rumpled informality of the image. These are the comforts of the familiar.

My mother died five years after the photograph was taken, but this is *the* photo, and she will forever remain for me the age she is in this picture. Looking at it, I register weight and heaviness, the three of us nestling into the hollows our bodies create, the weight of my head on my arm, of my elbow on her hip, of Ron's body on her breast, of her arm on my shoulder—all of that causing the sofa to sag a bit. We are grounded. We are family. "Our warmth is the result of the burning that goes on ceaselessly within our bodies," *The Book of Knowledge* explains, and the sharing of that warmth is everywhere in this photograph.

But then, just as I begin to feel less lost, I see it: a detail tossed nonchalantly into the picture. Looking hard at the upper left corner I notice, for the first time, a small wing shape on the sofa back, off toward the edge of the frame. What is that? I'm not sure at first, even after I lift the magnifying glass and look closely, but when I tilt the frame under a lamp, I can make out a familiar shape. It is the wing of a balsa glider, a *Jetfire*, like the one that sent me spinning in the downstairs den on the day that my mother died, and suddenly the image on the desktop beside me seems less grounded, less real, the bodies in the photograph becoming a composite of mere shapes on paper. We are not sitting on a sofa at all but are suspended weightless in space, and my mother is the centerpiece of this mobile pendent in air, claiming children for some underground dwelling in Never Never Never Land, the androgynous marionette hovering among the stars at the nursery window in a dangle of moving parts and hooks, floating forever away on gauzy wings with her lost boys under her arms.

Pencils in the house smell like perfume, and erasers, licked hard, are a smooth nut brown. The magazine rack, its wicker strands curling loose, spills over with old numbers while the new ones—56's and 57's—get thrown away. In every lamp only one bulb works. These objects remain framed and tinted as I think back on my childhood. An ivory elephant with a chipped tusk, beside it a mahogany one, the ball bat left out all night on the dewy lawn. Daily light enters and withdraws from this world in the mind. At night it is backlit like a dream. It never goes away. A pin glitters in the carpet. In the bedroom a tie is draped from the arm of a lamp, the ends neatly lined up as if that's where it belongs. All this, and more, and always too much, and never enough.

Familiar foes.

~   ~   ~

On a low bookshelf in my office rests a walnut stationery box from the American Cyanamid Company with the scene of a sunrise behind a barn and a cornfield carved into the lid. Cattle, hogs, and chickens graze on a hillside in the foreground of the carving above the words

127

"M. J. Harvey, Thirty Three Years of Excellence, 1950-1983." He was initially approached about the possibility of working with the company at a restaurant in Topeka before I was born, and, by the time he had finished, the arc of his career had taken him through top management positions. When I was going to college, he was under consideration for the presidency of the company, and when he was passed over for a younger man, began to plan his exit which consisted of a job he loved, entertaining clients by taking them goose hunting along the Delmarva Peninsula. My dad remained with Cyanamid twenty-one years after my mother killed herself and in many ways the company, to which he was wedded longer than he was married to either of his wives, was his life.

But the years just before my mother's death, when he moved from regional to district manager, were probably the ones that set the trajectory of his career and demanded the most of him. In 1954 my father was working long hours and "had put out more reports and letters since the first of the year than all the other men in the dept. combined." According to my mother, the head of Lederle at the time that my dad worked there in the mid-fifties was unable to go higher in the company which wanted to go in new directions, and, since the company ethos kept the pecking order of personnel in place, Cyanamid would only rarely "go around a boss to advance another man under him." My father's "only chance" according to my mother, was "to make a lateral move" to another division of the company, one with a robust future, and ride that wave upward. This was the testing ground. My mother called it the Cyanamid "Shuffle" in which the fate of the men—and at that time they were just men—depended on not getting placed in a dead-end position with a product line that was not growing.

My dad got his break in 1954 when a member of his division moved from Lederle to Fine Chemical Company, bringing "the cream of Lederle's top men" with him. When my father's supervisor at Lederle called Dad to his office to say he would not stand in my father's way as he made this shift, he spoke frankly to him. "I want you to know that I was not asked for this position." The person in charge "wanted you, personally." My mother and dad were grateful, and pleased with the offer. "It does mean a raise in pay but even more so the chance for advancement is at least in sight again." If my father had stayed in "the veterinary group he could have been pigeon-holed for years." My mother also saw it as a "moral victory" since she refused to participate in the usual rounds of "luncheons and bridge and dinners" with the bosses' wives that other company wives pursued. She felt relieved that Dad had succeeded "according to ability and work and not the social whirl."

What they could not foresee was the damage that moving high in the corporate chain would produce. The relocation, the purchase of a house, and above all the pressure to do well in the new situation would make the demands of the job, and the pressure that the job put on the family, worse. The higher Dad moved up into the company the tighter the squeeze. In 1957, when my father got another chance for a promotion and the opportunity to be regional manager in Chicago, he had already started construction on a new house in New Jersey which was moving slowly. They made the move anyway, to our place in Deerfield, Illinois, and my mother did not complain except to admit that the experience was "nerve-wracking." It was my father who took the brunt of all this maneuvering, she claimed. "Max is the one it is hardest on. He is traveling the territory all week and then dashing around to catch planes, etc on the weekend when travel becomes congested." In the end she saw the delay in getting the house finished as a blessing: "Maybe the wait is fortunate—with everything fluctuating so—it's hard to know what to do."

~ ~ ~

During this time of hectic change, my father bought a large, cross-sectional slab of black walnut three inches thick, twenty-six inches wide, and eighty inches long. "It was cut at such an angle across the trunk," my mother wrote, "that it afforded an elliptical shape." My dad sent it to a cabinet maker who planed it and made legs for a coffee table. Dad's task was to sand and finish it. "It will be quite a lot of work," my mother wrote, "but the grain is gorgeous and will not only be a pretty piece but also," she added, always aware of how hard it was for her to entertain Dad's colleagues and wives, "a conversational piece." My mother explained that Dad had been "talking to a Mr. Fee for several weeks" about it before making a purchase, and I suspect that he discovered it on one of their many road trips into the Hudson River Valley, especially given the legends that my mother associated with it. "It is said that George Washington paid off his soldiers under this tree," my mother explained proudly, and that "replica plaques were made for some lamps" cut from wood of the same tree.

Dad worked on the table when he could for a year and a half before our move to Illinois, retiring for hours at a time on weekends home from his business trips to sand, finish, and hand rub his project, and in October 1957 my mother could announce that he had devoted an entire weekend to it and was nearly done. "It is lovely and has a warm glow to the finish that only hand rubbing can give." It is true that the table, which sits in my step-mother's living room now, has a beautiful surface inviting to the touch made with many thin layers of polyurethane—a new product at the time—creating a thick but limpid coating that seems to magnify the grain. Most of his time was given to sanding, the first stage of his project, and I remember seeing him in a t-shirt and slacks under a bare light bulb smoking a cigarette, with one eye half shut against the smoke, sanding for hours to get the surface smooth.

I wonder what solace this solitary work on the coffee table gave him as the wood turned powdery from sanding and, later, when he carefully stroked the clear layers of urethane onto the surface of a piece of walnut some two-hundred years old so that it glowed like the water of a windless lake. What did he see, alone amid the commotion of my brother and me preparing for bed in another room, as he rubbed the surface of his project with soft cloths hour after hour? He finished the table just in time for our move, and I am sure that in its weight and natural beauty it seemed sturdy, rooted in reality in a way that the life of a corporate executive buffeted by the "Cyanamid Shuffle" could never be, but he must have also seen, as he leaned into each stroke of the cloth and felt the firm resistance of the wood to his imprint, the suggestion of a more portentous change in the swirling grain emerging from his reflection. No matter how glossy he made the surface, how bright and clear the image of his face glowed in the glass under the chamois, the wood grain only grew darker and more convoluted, the contour lines of the slab distorting the ghostly outline of the face of a familiar foe.

~ ~ ~

The word "familiar" suggests family life, but in its earliest occurrences in English it was combined with a word for an adversary, adding another layer of meaning to the cozy concept of the household: the familiar as a haven under threat from hostile forces. "O famuler fo," wrote Chaucer in "The Merchant's Tale" in 1385, the first example of the word in English literature, and "the false treason of his familier enemy" wrote Thomas More in *A Treatise on the Passion of Christ* the year before he was beheaded in 1535. The warm, interior hearth may feel snug, this etymology suggests, but it is in danger. It can be destroyed from within by sickness and contagion, hunger and woe, but it is also vulnerable to being violated from without. The door of the household can be kicked in, the men and boys killed, and the women and girls dragged out by the hair.

That sense of the family as a refuge from the world increased over time as family became more personal and intimate. During the reign of Queen Victoria, Alfred Lord Tennyson, who was surrounded by servants, lived in the bucolic setting of Farringford House on the western tip of the Isle of Wight, but, according to his biographer, Michael Thorn, photogravures of him playing with his children there popularized the idea of the family as a private, isolated refuge from a busy world. A renaissance in children's literature also helped establish the centrality of homey family life in the Victorian and Edwardian eras with writers such as Lewis Carroll, Kenneth Grahame, and A.A. Milne producing illustrated books that mothers and fathers could read to their children. It was during this age that J. M. Barrie launched Peter Pan, the boy threatened by Captain Hook, who is both father and enemy, the epitome of the familiar foe.

In my family, this sense of the familiar as a refuge was reinforced by my mother's familiar foes, depression and paranoia. Dad wanted a house that was open to the public with parties and games and entertainment, but since he was gone much of the time my mother controlled household affairs and set the tone of intimate isolation. After he remarried, it was common to find that my father and stepmother had weekend guests at the breakfast table while my dad, in slippers and a robe, flipped dollar cakes and cooked bacon and eggs on the stove. And when I was young, we would often at his insistence go on vacations with other families. For my mother, that way of life was an intrusion. "I'm not much of a gad about—rather like my own home," she wrote. For her, family was a way to withdraw from society into the cocoon of the family room, the room of familiar things, lit by a TV and the lamp-lit pages of *The Book of Knowledge*.

~ ~ ~

After the move to Illinois in 1958 my mother made a conscious effort to be happy. She "vowed to be patient, calm, and enjoy life." The declaration came after a return from a "grand week" in Kansas with her parents: "my visit with you opened my eyes and I thank you." She lamented the "eastern influence" of living in New York and saw the move to Illinois as a return to the Midwest and to her truer nature, one less concerned with focusing on the self. "Midwestern people are a finer grain," she claimed. Living in the East may have encouraged independence of thought, for which she was grateful. In the East you are able to "think for yourself and not be influenced by group thinking," but living there also made her lonely.

In Deerfield she hoped to be able to "meet more people." She backed off now from taking public positions—the economic debates of a nation entering the space race, for instance, "are beyond me," she wrote, and she still let my gregarious father take the lead socially: "as always with Max, we start circulating quickly. With me," she admits, "it would take forever." Much of the enthusiasm prompted by the move appears in retrospect to be trumped up. The letters are less candid emotionally after this point as she increasingly filters out bad news, and I am suspicious about that conversation in Kansas. What had my grandparents said that "opened her eyes"? Was this a friendly conversation about the possibilities created by a new move, or an intervention to right the course of a life that had become self-centered as a result of modern anxieties? Either way, she did see her first year back in the Midwest as liberating, writing that she had gotten back up to her old weight and "felt ten years younger."

"Have fun, and to heck with the trivial things," she declared, sweeping away her problems and adding a euphemistic dismissal that simply was not true: "I enjoy it that way."

The "years of uncertainty" about where they would eventually settle down had taken a toll, she believed, but the modern home in an "established" neighborhood promised to restore her confidence. She threw herself into housework with a renewed excitement and devoted herself to family activities. "Sunday was a wonderful day," she wrote in one letter from that year. "Very relaxed. Played in the back yard with the boys, putting up their trapeze, rings, and swing set. It was a beautiful day."

~ ~ ~

She loved the extravagant beauty of the ordinary. "The boys had been wanting some fish," she explained, "so we bought a small aquarium." We started with three guppies "Fannie, Flowie, and Cloie," the two neon tetras "Flash and Dash," and two angelfish. She named one of the angelfish "Tinkerbell," after the fairy in Peter Pan, but the other "died in a few hours so we didn't get it named."

My brother and I delighted in the guppies. Like the neon tetras which darted about in a choreographed unison the guppies were constant motion, but the dance was more chaotic and playful. They liked to poke other fish with their snouts and peck them with their mouths, sometimes taking a nip of the tail. The tetras had a neon stripe which made them fun to watch, but the guppies had a spectacular glow, "every color combined into one harmonious whole," *The Book of Knowledge* explains. Their bodies were translucent—the shadowy outlines of internal organs visible in the light—and the tails waved in the water like golden veils. We watched in awe as a mother guppy gave birth, a spray of fry dropping from her black belly, while a male guppy with a wide and sweeping tail swooped below to eat a few.

My mother thought the guppies had killed the first angel fish. She heard that they are cannibalistic and they did seem aggressive. Her suspicions received confirmation when one of the neons died. "Friday night, Dash just disappeared—not a trace." She placed the guppies "on probation" and announced that if any more fish disappeared, the guppies "would lose their happy home." In the end, the aquarium was fulfilling its main function which, my dad explained, was to teach us lessons in death, and we often took our places at the side of the toilet bowl and looked on solemnly as the named and unnamed were flushed away.

My mother loved the angelfish and neons and hoped "to keep some of the pretty ones alive," but the beginning was rocky. "We have 2 left of 4 pretty ones," she wrote. She planned to buy more but Dad convinced her to wait until our bowl was "better established." In the end, only the guppies survived, little pirates patrolling their small aquatic domain in satin vests, no one to peck but each other as their numbers swelled. We watched them float in and about a plastic treasure chest that opened and closed as it released air into the tank. The little corsairs liked to ride the bubbles to the surface wriggling and glittering all the way up, while we watched in wonder. Afterward they floated without effort down to the stones staring back with their beaded eyes, daring us, it seemed, to put another "pretty one" in their midst.

Tinkerbell did not last long. No amount of clapping saved her. "The Angel Fish is noted for its haughty, dignified manner," *The Book of Knowledge* explains, but that does not describe the way ours looked in the tank. She was beautiful with her long, smooth pelvic fins that sometimes dragged along the stones like the hem of a bridal gown. From the side, she had a wide, wing-shaped body with feathery dorsal and ventral fins that came to sharp points above and below, but when she turned to face us she was so thin that she nearly disappeared. To me she looked "pretty" as my mother wrote, but also vulnerable and terrified, blowing small kisses our way, as she glided among her predators. Most of the time she floated in the center of the tank, buffeted by currents and afraid of the darker corners, suspended and still and slowly rotating, awaiting her Captain Hook. The guppies probably did not do her in. They were cannibalistic, not predatory. No, some internal compulsion or disease, nurtured in their warm aquatic home, was to blame. Flash, like Dash, no doubt met his doom by leaping out of the claustrophobic world of his tank, wriggling to a dusty grave under the sofa. Tail rot or ich probably killed the rest. One way or another, death arrived, and we found Tinkerbell crumpled on the aquarium floor one morning like a tossed hanky, content, it seemed, that the worst was over at last.

~ ~ ~

One time, when I was probably ten my mother caught my friend Chris and me looking at pictures in a *Playboy* magazine. Chris and Jamie Robinson who lived next door were about my age. "Steve has found a real bosom friend in Chris," my mother wrote. "They both like the same type of things. Sending messages by flash cards through the upstairs bedroom windows—working out codes and doing chemistry experiments—studying the world globe, etc." I remember the flash cards most. Our houses were side-by-side about twenty-five feet apart and the upstairs window of their two-story Tudor place was about the same height as the one in the bedroom of our wood frame split-level. The "cards" were actually the inside cardboard that came home with my dad's shirts from the laundry. On them we would write brilliant messages such as "See You Outside." I would hold up my sign and Chris or Jamie answered with corresponding brilliance.

"OK!"

We also created our own telephone and strung it between the houses. The plan came from *The Book of Knowledge*, of course. "If you take two tin cups without bottoms, fasten a piece of parchment, or even tough paper, tightly over one end of each, make a tiny hole in the center of each piece and stretch a wire between them, you have a telephone." *The Book* added that you could easily stretch it so that you could "talk with your friend across the street, or in the next house." My mother threw herself into these projects as the main supplier of materials. After I wrinkled a pile of Dad's shirts getting out sheets of cardboard backing, she started saving them for us and suggested we use paper cups instead of metal ones for our phones since none of us had tin cups. She also came up with an idea for getting the string in both windows when she saw us trying to throw one end tied to a rock up to the window of Chris's room. Fearing that we would break the pane, she came running out of the house drying her hands, and told us to drop another string from

Chris's window, tie it, and pull the string up. We thought she was a genius.

The trick with the telephone was to keep the line taut. Chris would call me on the regular phone to say it was time to talk which, in retrospect, was pretty ridiculous in itself. I would sit on a chair at the window and pull the cord on the phone until it was tightly drawn and say "See you outside."

He would say, "OK!"

"This simple toy will not carry the waves very far," *The Book* explains, "but from a beginning like this the wonder of the telephone has come." We were tapping into a Machine Age miracle, and our enthusiasm for the modern showed in the language of our play. When Chris and I tried unsuccessfully to fly a kite together, we borrowed our vocabulary from the space program. We had quite a struggle getting it "launched," I told my mother after the first try, and when we did finally get it aloft, the string tangled in a tree bringing the kite down with a crash in the neighbor's yard. After I retrieved the damaged kite and brought it home I announced to her that the launch was successful this time, but we failed to get the kite "in orbit."

In many ways the familiar pleasures of the first year in Deerfield, the setting for my mother's final act, do seem wondrous. The neighbors who lived in the house behind the Robinson's flooded their backyard each winter. It took most of a day but when they were done the entire lawn was a frozen lake of ice that lasted all winter in the cold air north of Chicago. On the weekends they played music from an upstairs window, and turned on lights that they had strung around the makeshift rink, and all of the kids in the neighborhood came to skate in lazy circles under the yellow glow. I had trouble getting my laces tight enough—I wobbled on my blades—so my mom tied them really tight. I looked down at the part in her hair as she knelt at my feet, pulling the laces hard and letting me put a finger on the first lace cross as she made the loops and tied the knot. Bundled up in a heavy coat, I hobbled across the back yard, scrambled over the fence at the stile, and joined my friends making lazy circles across the glittering homemade lake.

It may have been a year or two after we moved to Deerfield that Chris brought the *Playboy* to the front stoop of our house and we flipped through the pages of the magazine. I don't remember what the pictures looked like—the usual fifties cheesecake, I guess—though I know that I was interested. I had a little girlfriend who followed me home from school. She had olive skin and dark hair cut in bangs. We never talked, but when I took a detour at a construction site, she followed behind as we walked over planks between walls and on plywood-covered puddles, with me picking up metal slugs punched out of electrical outlets along the way and putting them in my pockets like coins. Eventually we wandered back to the sidewalk and went home, never touching or talking the whole way. In a letter, my mom mentions that I had begun carrying a comb in my back pocket about that time.

When my mother discovered Chris and me looking at *Playboy*, we knew we were in trouble, but to my surprise she did not get angry. She asked Chris where he got the magazine, and he said that it belonged to his father. She told him that he should take it home, and she would call his mother. Then my mother did something that remains one of the most vivid of the few memories I have of the two of us alone together. She took me into the house and pulled out the large glossy art books with paintings by the Impressionists. "A woman's body is beautiful," she told me. I'm almost sure those were her words. The female form, she explained, was the most noble subject of the greatest artists. And together on the couch—the one covered in geometrical shapes that had made its way from Nanuet to Deerfield—the two of us looked at Impressionist paintings of nude women, including "Bather with Long Hair" by Renoir, a portrait of a naked woman up to her thighs in water with pale skin, young breasts, rounded hips, and long chestnut hair lit by the sun. The young woman's face is expectant, maybe hopeful, and her body plump with promise, though her dark eyes gaze ahead, soulful and a little sad. It was her breasts that held my guilty stare, the one on her left framed by thick twists of brown hair and the other facing straight on, bold and inviting as a peach. I don't remember the exact words for the rest of my mother's little speech, but she said that I would grow up one day and one of my greatest joys would be to love the body of a woman. She spoke to me directly and plainly, without embarrassment, as we sat together turning the large pages of the folio in the afternoon light. It was natural for a boy my age to be curious about girls, she said, but such beauty required respect, and a magazine like *Playboy* cheapened women. It was not worthy of them or me. The room was filled with sunlight and the sheers on the picture window beside us glowed white as she talked. When she finished she left me alone in the room, the shimmering pages of the art book open on the coffee table in front of me.

~ ~ ~

One summer my family took a fishing trip to a cabin on Lake Superior in Grand Marais, Minnesota. Sterling Brackett, one of Dad's senior associates, had the rental next door and flew in by plane, but we arrived, after a long, hot drive, in the Buick and parked beside our shingled cabin right on the lake. A grassy path led down to a dock with a small boat attached. My brother and I ran down to the landing, clamored over wooden planks, looked out on a cove of calm, blue water lined with evergreens on the far shore, and glanced over the edge of the dock at our rippling reflections. When Dad joined us he pointed to the lake and said that it was loaded with walleyed pike.

That year Dad came in at 130% of his sales quota despite a recession, but the success came at a price for the family since he was often gone for weeks at a time. This trip was to be a chance for father and mother and sons to get closer. One day was just for me. Dad woke me at sunrise while my mother and younger brother slept and led me down to the boat. As usual when he went hunting or fishing, he was up before dawn and had the gear and provisions all ready, right down to the sandwiches packed in a cooler, and we spent the day on the lake. After Dad cut the motor on the small boat, we floated along the shore, the mountains and water still, the peace broken only occasionally by the shrill cry of a gull, the splash of a leaping fish, or the low rumblings of our movements in the boat. Dad taught me to look over the gunwale for walleye, mysterious shapes suspended in water perfectly clear down to the bottom, and to cast a line near shallow rocky areas and weedy edges where the elusive fish were most apt to hide. "The walleyed pike or pike perch," *The Book of Knowledge* explains, "may grow to be as much as three feet long and weigh as much as twenty-five pounds, but most specimens are much smaller." Dad reached into his large, blue fishing kit and carefully selected a jig for his line, lifting it slowly out of the tangle of hooks and pinches of hair and feathers in the top tray. He showed me how to tie a clinch knot and hook the minnows, but he attached a bobber to my line to make it easier for me to spot the catch. When I got a nibble he made me wait until I felt a strong strike and the bobber went completely under. By midday we had made our catch—my dad let me lift the stringer loaded with flapping bodies out of the water for a good look—and headed back to the cabin, the blue hills surrounding the lake receding into the horizon behind us, swallowed up by the trees of our small cove.

Once back at the landing, I ran to the cabin for my mother. She set down her book and walked the path behind me to see what we had caught, and Dad lifted one of the big ones in his hands, showing it to her. "Thanks to their great spiny fins," *The Book of Knowledge* explains, "the perch are audacious," and Dad treated the flexing body of the walleye with respect. He held it firmly as it squirmed under his thumbs, the sharp dorsal fin stiff and erect and pointing away, rising above a dark green back and golden body mottled with brown. The belly shone white. Walleye get their name from the large shallow retina of their eyes that glitters iridescently like tinfoil, and as my dad held it we could see the colors play in the shifting of light along the golden iris.

"It's dinner," my father said, looking at my mother.

"It's beautiful," I hear her saying as she made a gesture to touch it but held back. "Before it comes in the house," she insisted, "you'll clean it."

"It's the price you pay for a day on the lake," my father explained as we walked back to the landing, the stringer of flopping walleye in his fist, although I think he loved all aspects of fishing including cleaning up. We lay the bundle on the grassy bank while he got his knife and a bucket, and I watched as the fish would struggle, slap their tail fins on the ground, and gasp, drowning in air. One at a time, he whacked the head against a rock stunning the fish, causing its body to stiffen and twist involuntarily. He scraped away the scales with the edge of the blade and cut off the head and tail. Turning the body over, he slit open the belly, producing a black line against the pearly-white flesh, and scooped out the insides— multicolored guts and internal organs—and threw the offal into a bucket.

142

"We had a wonderful time. The cool brisk air is very invigorating," my mother wrote. "Had a grand time."

"Your turn," Dad said to me after he had cleaned a few, making me reach inside the slit belly to pull out the slimy innards. In one fish we found roe in a bundle and I showed it to Dad, who pulled back the flesh with the tip of his knife and said, "Look at that." He pointed with his knife to a separate bucket. "Save that." At times, as I dug inside a cold body, the fish seemed to shudder or twist in my hand. It's alive, I thought, but my dad assured me the fish was well beyond feeling any pain, pointing again with his knife to the decapitated heads in the bucket. My guilty glance followed the blade, but, when I looked inside the pail, all I could see among the snouts, mandibles, gills, and organs were the eyes of the walleyes, animated by the light of the sun, staring at me accusingly from their beautiful and empty shallowness.

It's the price you pay.

~ ~ ~

On the way back from our fishing trip we stopped at Crystal Cave, a large underground cavern near Spring Valley, Wisconsin. "It is quite spectacular," my mother wrote. "The boys loved the 1-hour tour." The cave was discovered in 1881 when a sixteen-year-old farm boy named William Vanasee chased a squirrel down a sink hole. According to the promotional material, the boy told his brother George about the find and the two of them returned with a rope and lantern and lowered themselves into the opening to explore. It led them into a cave that was later discovered to be an enormous underground cavern of limestone, sandstone, and dolomite, sedimentary rocks known as the Prairie du Chien formation.

We entered the cave through a wide, public walkway, passing the original entrance that the Vanasee brothers had shimmied through. The cavern was strung with electric lights giving the passageways a subterranean glow. Dripping flowstone ran in sensuous sheets that rippled like reptilian hide along the walls and crawl spaces dotted with stalactites and stalagmites opened like crocodile maws on either side of us. The guide—probably a college student home for the summer—gave us a simple rule for remembering the difference between the two formations. Stalactites, she said, "hold tight to the ceiling" and stalagmites "reach up with all their might."

The tour culminated in the great chamber where we were presented with a formation that the guide described as if it were one of the wonders of the world: a round stalagmite. The shape rose out of a shelf of stone into a neat sphere, like a golf ball on a tee, "a rarity" our guide assured us. For good luck we were encouraged to reach into the formation and touch it, so one by one we filed past the opening and rubbed the cool, rounded stone. Some may think that "a cave is just a natural cavity beneath the earth's surface," *The Book of Knowledge* explains in a section called "Wonderful Caverns," but "we all know it to be much more than that. It is mystery, beauty and adventure."

~ ~ ~

The last few letters from my mom were giddy with exciting news, and in the one I'm holding now she is ebullient. Dad had been promoted to Regional Manager in Cyanamid and, since he had convinced the "brass," as my mom called his bosses, to divide the region, Dad could remain in Chicago and the family would not have to move. After redoing the kitchen in Formica tile and finishing off the basement as a downstairs den, my parents were pleased with this turn of events, and my mom seems genuinely happy about remaining in the Midwest, close to her parents.

My father entertained the New York brass while they were in Chicago as only he could do. He put them up in the venerable Palmer House downtown and they dined at Caruso's. Mom and Dad threw a dinner party—"13 of us in all" my mother wrote—and "everything worked out perfectly." I was ten at the time and played guitar and sang and "was very entertaining." As usual, I "beamed." Once the decision was made in Dad's favor, the head of the company invited my mother to join the weekend celebrations. "After getting the babysitter, I scrambled to straighten the house after party guests," she wrote, "get food ready, pack, and rush to the train—just barely made it," but her tone is excited rather than harried. She and my dad attended the company's cocktail party at five o'clock, dined with clients at Chez Paree, and took in a show starring Joey Bishop. All the while my mother was fighting "a terrible cold" and both she and my father ended the week exhausted, but the letter, like all of the final letters, is remarkable in that she never expresses her usual apprehension about entertaining and seems confident, rather than insecure, about her ability to handle these demands. Everything, she announced, "turned out successful!"

A few weeks later, after the whirl of events began "calming down" my parents decided to spend some time with just my brother and me. "We felt a kid's day was definitely in order," Mom wrote. They took us to see the St. Louis Cardinals play the Chicago Cubs. We had seats behind first base so we could get "a good look at Stan Musial," the celebrated home-run hitter for the St. Louis Cardinals, but I was becoming a Cubs fan and was mesmerized by the Chicago star, Ernie Banks. "It was a beautiful, warm day," and a good game, "the Cub's winning 4-0."

After the game Dad took us to Schulien's, a neighborhood bar and restaurant, near Revere Park in north Chicago. The restaurant had been at this spot since 1886 and became popular in the 1920's when the celebrated magician Harry Blackstone began to do tricks for customers. When Matt Schulien took over, he, and later his sons, continued the tradition by doing close-up card tricks at the tables, many of the tricks invented by the elder Schulien himself. By 1960, when we came for our dinner, Matt Schulien had retired and rarely performed for the customers, but he still lived upstairs and my dad's powers of persuasion accompanied by a ten-dollar tip brought the old man to our table to do his most famous trick.

It is one of the dozen vivid memories that I had before the letters stirred up so many more. I remember looking for a reference to it when I first read through the boxes of correspondence and being disappointed that it wasn't there. Later, I found another box misplaced in a file cabinet in my office containing a few stray letters, and there it was, the story of the card trick at Schulien's.

Matt Schulien was large with a wide face, big smile, ruddy complexion, and hair combed back in a silver wave. He stepped slowly down the stairs gripping the rail and crossed the room by grabbing onto chair backs, but he made his entrance in style wearing a white shirt and a tie and acknowledging the customers with a nod as he passed. He told my mother that he was "3 score and 10," proud of his longevity. His breathing came hard, and he had to pause a few minutes after he slumped down in his chair to catch his breath, wheezing at the end of each sentence, but as soon as the trick started he became the consummate entertainer. He offered up a wide smile as he shuffled and cut the cards deftly and his eyes sparkled with mischief.

"He sits right at the table," Mom explained, "but is so good at sleight of hand" that he easily fooled us. My brother "watched and reacted with glee—he became convinced that the cards were magic." I was old enough to know it was a trick, and studied the magician's hands in vain for any clue of how it was done. "Steve watched closely and was amazed that he couldn't catch him." His final, celebrated trick began with me choosing a card from the deck, showing it to my family, and putting it back in the deck. The magician asked my dad to cut and shuffle the cards as many times as he liked, those high arching shuffles my dad could do while holding a cigarette in his mouth and squinting with one eye, and when Dad finished, he set the deck back on the table. The magician squared the cards and handed me a tack. He asked me to inspect it carefully before placing it on the deck and when I was done, he scooted his chair awkwardly away from the table, lifted the deck, tack and all, high into the air, his large body stretching back as he raised his arm, and hurled the cards against the wall. Hearts and spades, clubs and diamonds spun everywhere and splatted in a wild array, but when the flurry of red and black tumbled to the floor, one card, the ten of clubs, remained pinned to the wall. The card I had chosen. Afterward, my dad found "two 10 of clubs in an old deck and had the gentleman autograph them for the boys." It was a "wonderful day" and "all enjoyed it," Mom wrote, adding with some pride that the cards were "tacked up in the recreation room now."

Reading the letters straight through, it is clear that my mother's disease was both chronic and cyclical. "I look so good and feel cheerful again," she writes in 1954, after one of the worst years of anxiety over my brother's eyes, explaining that "things are looking up after our year of blackness." At bridge one of her friends said to my dad that "she had never seen Bobbie look prettier or happier." When she is well, she dismisses the sick person she has been as a stranger whom she barely recognizes. "I actually feel like myself," she writes, and "seem to be blooming." And yet, in these letters of hopefulness she feels miserably guilty for her lapses during her sickness. "I was negligent about writing when you needed me so much after grandmother's passing away," she admits to her mother. She claims that her illness should be "no excuse" for her failures, and that she has "no right to ever be that way," and in an afterthought squeezed between the lines offers this forlorn admission: "I feel so badly about so many things this past year."

In 1956 after my grandfather's stroke, the blackness returned and when it passed she once again believed that she was on top of things. "I truly feel wonderful this summer," she writes in October of 1957. She stopped taking Miltown, the drug of choice in the mid-fifties for depression, though she credited it with her "return to good health," and is proud of the fact that she had gotten her weight up to 115. "Lord knows I am happy to be myself again," she wrote, but all of this effusive cheerfulness may have been her way of apologizing for the pain she had caused others, especially her parents, and her insistence that it will not happen again, more a sign of her resolve than an honest assertion of happiness. She was writing when she felt good enough and happy enough to be convincing, but she seems so defensive about her past that the motive for all this good cheer is not clear.

A close reading of the letters suggests that her illness lingered in her, even when a crisis was over, and was never very far away or completely subdued. She had been taking some form of tranquilizing drug like Miltown on and off since 1948 when Dr. Jackman prescribed medication to reduce her moodiness, the length of time a clue that her illness was a constant in her life. But it is in the letters themselves, especially the ones before 1958 when she was still frank and honest, that her happy experiences were laced with darker feelings.

In a typical letter written on October 23, 1957, my grandmother's birthday, my mother, enjoying one of her happier times, was on an emotional see-saw. She had bought two new dresses along with silver jewelry for a dinner party with some of the company people from Kansas City, which "gave her a lift," and she wanted to wear the blue one. "It does more for me with its vivid color." Unfortunately, the occasion called for the "grey as a basic dress" so despite her anxiety about often looking drab she wore the more plain dress which "looked nice" but required "more make-up." The ambivalence continues when she thanks her mother for being concerned about her loneliness when my father was away.

The "concern" came on "the right day" suggesting that my mother had been blue when my father was on a trip. "I was a little disgruntled about waiting for something to happen," she complained vaguely. My grandmother recommended that she call on those days which my mother wrote was "very thoughtful" and "very sweet" even as she declined the offer: "I would rather call you when happy." She added a parenthetical "ha" after the word happy which she often did when she was not really joking.

After the move to Deerfield, she rarely brings up depression again in the letters. The hints of gloom are gone and much of the melancholy disappears. On July 16, 1958, the change is apparent. She writes about my Little League baseball team, playing golf with dad, the Rock Island Rocket (the train line that still ran from Chicago through Manhattan, Kansas), the family trip to Lake Superior, and the Senate racketeering committee hearings investigating crime in Chicago. There are problems: we lost the ball game because of a bad call by the ump, she certainly did not help my father's golf game since this was her first time out, and Chicago corruption was, apparently, spreading to nearby towns, but none of these complaints has a personal edge to it. She is even able to joke about her weight—that she was up a dress size and for the first time had to watch her eating which tickled my dad who was always on a diet. I know that her depression did not go away, and the horrible nighttime fights with my father continued and got worse and that the outcome four years after the move to Deerfield was suicide, but in the last few years the demons are kept out of the envelopes.

The letters served as a reminder of her best self and created an exemplary biography for her to imagine and, when she could, live up to. They allowed her to be the loving mother she described and gave her a path to follow as she picked her way through the many fears that her paranoia had raised in her. In part, they worked their magic by allowing her to pay attention to a world outside of herself, so in the letter about the Little League game, golf, and the Rock Island Rocket she included a paragraph about animals. "We have some rabbits and squirrels that play in our yard. In New York it was the chipmunk. They have such lovely coats of fur—all this good grass." Reading that I know my mother has set aside for the moment her melancholic self-absorption to make room for a different emotion. "We love the animals," she explained. The letters helped her, just as they have helped me understand her, by making her life richer and fuller. It is when they stopped that she was in trouble.

~ ~ ~

I do not know what the final hours of my mother's life were like—how could I? She was alone, and the boxes of letters that taught me so much about her stopped for most of her last year and are, on this subject, silent. Perhaps she thought back on the suicide of Wilson Lane, the neighbor in Dodge City, who parked his car near the Ford County Lake and stuffed a tube up the tailpipe, but even if that horrible event planted a seed, it doesn't clarify much. His motives were inscrutable to her because outwardly he had "everything to live for." In the end there is no way to know for certain why someone does an act as private, desperate, and violent as a successful suicide. It is the black hole around which a universe of loved ones spins like debris.

I know that she was in part the victim of her position as a woman in America during the 1940's and 50's. It is hard to judge the effect of leaving her career in nursing except to say that the problems that haunted her for the rest of her life first appear in the letters after she decides to leave her training, marry my dad, and set up house in Dodge City. There is an almost palpable sense of her world closing in on her as the possibility of work outside the home slipped away, leaving little but dreary days of household duties ahead. Her attempts to work with my dad at the veterinary clinic seem almost pathetic as she did bookkeeping and occasionally gave inoculations to the animals, and his suggestion to pay her to wake him up—offered as a joke—is not funny when seen in light of her struggle to wake herself up in a world that saw cure as sedation.

When she first went to Dr. Jackman, a good-hearted physician locked into the assumptions of his time, his suggestion for her depression and loneliness, aside from drugs and more time with her husband, was to have a baby. I do believe that she took delight in her children. The letters, even the ones describing her gloomiest paranoid anxieties, are filled with her sense that my brother and I made her life fuller, but her role as corporate wife—that particularly insidious version of the fifties trap for women marked by small talk and innuendo, chain-smoking, passive-aggressive strategies for promoting your man, and an endless string of cocktail parties galled her. Above all, she detested the phoniness, the insincerity of corporate life, a game which she refused to play. Unfortunately she was required to stay on the field, drink and cigarette in hand, and smile, and rack her brains for something clever to say.

Still, I don't think that the explanation for her suicide can be entirely the result of her position as a woman in society. Many women suffered in this way and did not buy a large-bore gun, drive out to a park, and shoot themselves. Her problems admit sociological explanations, but those explanations are not sufficient for understanding her unique psychological agony. She wanted relief from a mind filled with paranoia and anxiety, the legacy of her father that took a particularly virulent and vicious form of depression in her. She had just gone through a round of counseling and drugs and electroshock therapy, and none of that had helped. If she suspected another year of blackness coming on, triggered by my father's infidelity, then she might have felt numb enough to put herself to death.

~ ~ ~

"Triggered by my father's infidelity"—what does that mean? When I was around five or six, and the family was living in Nanuet, my father fell through the ceiling. It was Christmastime and he was in the attic gathering up decorations that they stored there. In my mind he is wearing a white shirt and tie, so maybe he had gone to get the decorations before heading off to work. My mother and I were in the living room when it happened. First a shoe poked through—his leg dangling above us comically for a moment as my mother and I rushed into the hallway—and then his entire large body came crashing down through the sheetrock, broken strips of plaster everywhere. He landed on his feet, legs buckling a bit, and held out his arms as if to steady himself.

My mother let out a cry, but I laughed at the sight of my father disheveled, disoriented, covered in a white powder and staggering in the hallway. I'm not sure how he reacted to my insolence, but I suspect that he was angry. Once she knew that he was all right, my mother whisked me aside and while Dad cleaned himself up lectured me. "Your father is a great man," she said. "A success and a leader." She told me that he had risen quickly to positions of responsibility in his company, worked hard to support our family, and deserved our respect. She insisted that I apologize to him and told me that I would be lucky to be "half the man" that he was. It is the phrase—"half the man"—that sticks in my mind even when so much else about her is vague and indistinct. I know she said it.

My mother believed that she and dad were complete opposites, but she respected him, and I think that the thought of losing him filled her with anxiety because his leaving her for another woman served as a reminder of her own emptiness. She spent most of her time when he was gone waiting. And I know, when he burst into the house after a long business trip, my brother and I ran across the room and threw our arms around him knowing that when he was home the house would be filled with laughter and excitement again. Once, when he came home from a trip to Las Vegas, he and my mother woke me up in the middle of the night so that I could listen to a Shelley Berman comedy album that he had bought at Caesar's Palace, and even though I didn't get most of the jokes, I could lean against my father, knowing he was home, and listen to his laughter—and the laughter that his presence awakened in my mother.

So when my mother figured out the truth of his affair, I'm sure that she and Dad had one of their loud fights choreographed to the sound track of jazz, but I also suspect that when he was gone afterwards—to work, or back to St. Louis—her anger was tempered by the blankness, the tedium of her nightly gloom, and her own sense of failure. How could she, wrapped in the veils of her depression, hope to hold onto this man who turned heads when he walked into a room.

So my father takes some of the blame for what happened that day, but not all, because that would be too easy. It would let all of us off of the captain's hook. Furious as she was with him, I suspect that she, in the end, didn't blame him. She did not kill herself when she learned about my father's mistress which led to drunken nights swaying in front of the record console and to my grandparents' sudden arrival at our house. She waited until the day that Dad left the family for good after she had dropped him off at the train station and an endless emptiness swept in his wake.

Yes, she was in despair as she drove to a gun shop that morning to pick out a large bore pistol and a box of cartridges, charging them to my father, but something beyond his infidelity had thrust this decision on her. She drove twenty-five miles to the park in Lake Forest with the gun probably in the seat beside her, the kind of gun that my father used to shoot rattlesnakes and taught her, no doubt, how to fire. She pulled into a secluded area of the park, followed at a distance by a patrolman who spied her and was suspicious. She parked the car and opened the box of bullets beside her. I picture her fanning them out across the seat next to her, filling the chambers one by one with the heavy slugs. I like to think that she fell back into her own seat for a moment looking into the grove of trees ahead at a sight that in the past had brought solace, comfort, and a sense of possibility. I doubt if she had much energy left to spend on thoughts of Dad after weeks of fighting. Maybe she thought of her dad, her soul mate in depression, and her mother, her dearest confidante, both of whom were behind at the house waiting anxiously.

But I believe, knowing her as well as I do now, that she also thought of us. Her "boys." Ronnie who filled her heart with gladness and made her laugh even in times of despair, and me, the one who sang in a choir, played guitar for guests, and beamed with curiosity while holding a volume of *The Book of Knowledge* in his lap. When my dad left my mother, he was leaving us behind as well and did not plan to return. It is a joy, she wrote once, for them "just to be with their dad." Happy, smart, successful—he was the embodiment of hope. It may be true that after her death my grandmother mounted a small campaign to gain custody over us, but if so my dad fought back, and in the end we remained with him. My mother knew what he would do. Children are not to blame, of course, but the fear in a mother of being unable to raise them, of loving them but being a danger to them, the paranoia that she had nothing to offer their innocent lives but her disease and year after year of blackness—well, that for her was reason enough. With her out of the picture, Dad would take us back and raise us in a gregarious household which, by and large, he did. She imagined a life for us alone with her and her wraithlike gloom, surrounded by the familiar foes of her depression and paranoia, and realized that she just could not put herself or us through that.

Perhaps as she was loading the gun she saw in the rearview the patrol car parked down the road, precipitating final action. Quickly she snapped shut the chamber as my father had taught her and, hiding the pistol in her skirt, opened the door of the Buick. "She stepped out of the car" and shot herself. "Bam," my stepmother said. My mother was acting quickly before someone stopped her and before she stopped herself. The fact that this policeman might keep her from doing the hard but necessary thing may have cinched the deal. Perhaps the patrolman stepped out of his car and shouted something to her, but it was too late. She lifted the gun.

"Bam."

~ ~ ~

And what about the hours before she left the house? I have no idea, and that is a time that mattered. It was a Thursday in the morning. The TV was on and Dave Garroway, who would retire from his morning show in a month, was probably delivering the news. Things were heating up in Cuba and one report on the wire services said that an invasion was imminent. I imagine that I bounded down the steps two at a time in my pajamas the way I always did, making airplane sounds and holding the *Jetfire* balsa wood flyer in my fingertips, and sat down to eat a breakfast of Special K, my favorite. Since Dad was about to go on a trip and Mom would have to drive him in, I'm certain the morning was hectic. All of the terrible words that had to be spoken were probably said by then, and now the challenge was to get Dad to the station on time.

He wore a gray suit—well, I assume gray since it almost always was—and he lumbered down the steps lugging his suitcase that bumped, as usual, against the narrow stairway. Mom followed behind in a—well, it's an April morning in Chicago, so let's give her the plain blue skirt and blouse with the white jacket and paisley scarf combination she liked to wear on chilly days. She also wears sunglasses to hide whatever has been going on with her eyes. Fumbling in her purse, she searches for keys as she walks down the steps following Dad, and at the landing finds them at last and snatches them up with her hand. Ready to go. The only way she will get out this door is to act as if she is following the routine.

There is the say-goodbye-to-your-father moment. He bends down on one knee and my brother and I give him a hug unaware that he is abandoning us, but there is a deeper irony that he knows only dimly if at all. He isn't leaving for good—*she* is—an irony that my mother knows and my grandmother is sure of, and that everyone except my brother and me and maybe my dad suspect. I picture Grandma and Grandpa in the room sitting stonily. They never had many words to say to their son-in-law, and they have run out of words for their daughter. They have given up, consoling themselves at night, in the flat, plain-speak of Kansas by whispering: "They have to work this out for themselves."

It doesn't work out.

What I wonder about but can never know are the ominous clues that I missed, but might have caught, the indications that I, at the age of eleven, could have seen. Clues of the double treachery that would have allowed me to stop that awful day. Did my dad linger a little longer over his hug and pat on the back believing that this was it, guilty about his act of paternal betrayal? Did he pause and look about the room to say goodbye to the house that he had bought and renovated? Did my grandmother let out an uncontrollable sob that would have been a clue to my mother's intentions? Or turn away suddenly hiding her face? Did a tear, quickly wiped away, start to work its way down my grandfather's craggy cheek?

What did I miss in the tension of that moment?

"Wait," I wish I had said, rushing in front of my parents and their suitcases and pursed lips, holding my skinny arms out blocking the door.

And my mother's face. What did I miss there? For many years when we were little boys my mother bathed Ron and me together. She ran warm water over us with a cloth and laughed when we splashed water in her face as she bent over us. Surely she bent over us now in the same way, and looked me in the face, and said goodbye. Or be strong. Or I love you. I have no memory of those final words, but if she did say anything, I should have heard an ache in her voice. Or was the clue—the hint that I missed—non-verbal? Did she hold my face a moment too long in her two hands and, lifting away her sunglasses, look into my eyes from the darkened sockets of hers, and if so, how could I miss that? And if she did not signal her final departure in any way and played the part stoically, just to get out the door, I should have felt a lifetime of sadness welling up and held in check by the flimsiest of excuses: "hurry, we'll miss the train." I should have noticed *some*thing and raced between them and blocked their path. Isn't that why I wrote this book of knowing and wondering? Knowing she will die, and that there is nothing I can do to stop her, I want to create the characters anew, catch the clues this time, re-imagine my world like a conjurer, and change the outcome of the story. I want to be the boy who slams open the door and runs out into the street as the Buick pulls away waving his arms shouting "No!"

But I can't.

She won't let me.

She is doing this in part *for* me, I know now.

So even in this version of her tale I stand beside my brother at the storm door in my pajamas and wave, Grandma and Grandpa behind us, as she and Dad walk down the path to the car for the last time together, Dad lifting his suitcase into the trunk and Mom opening the driver's side door without looking back.

After my mother died and my father remarried, the new family moved to New Jersey. I was twelve by then, and my brother and I lived with our new sister in a split-level in the suburbs of Trenton, not far from the Princeton headquarters of American Cyanamid. I was in seventh grade, and the memories of those years, unlike the ones before that time, come flooding back with ease. My newly acquired older sister was pretty and popular with lots of friends and she took on, as a personal challenge, the task of socializing me for which I am forever thankful. I was a loner and a misfit after my mother's death—the "sensitive one" my father told everyone—but I also yearned, by nature, to break out of that isolation. I was as much my father's child, after all, as my mother's, and in the end I secretly enjoyed the Saturday night that all of my sister's girlfriends cornered me in the laundry room and showered me with kisses.

Still I sought out places where I could be alone, often not knowing why, and have never been able to give myself over entirely to the social life. I rarely thought of my mother directly, a fact that baffles me now. Some self-protecting part of my nature, reinforced by the family's silence, turned the subject of her life and death into a taboo during my adolescence, and I instinctively knew not to ask about it, not to talk about it, and eventually not to think about it. My wife tells me that when I first mentioned my mother's death to her I said that "she might have committed suicide." Occasionally I visited my grandmother in Kansas but even there a Midwestern code of restraint wrapped the subject up in the gauze of discretion, and later, after I married and my wife and I tried to visit Kansas more often, my grandmother had happily remarried and, when she talked about my mother at all, preferred to do so with Barbara rather than me.

But I am convinced, despite the silence, that my mother was never far from my mind. I felt drawn toward solitude. In junior high school I rode my bike for hours alone, and when I played basketball, I sought out empty courts. Activities that were social for others, such as playing the guitar and singing, I used as an excuse to be alone and often stayed in my room by myself crooning long, plaintive ballads by folk singers that were popular then. When my parents bought a house on the Jersey shore, I preferred the deck to the beach, and when I was fifteen, took a job as a dishwasher in a restaurant where I fell hopelessly in love with a waitress who was a college student five years older than I and spent most of my time pining away. I may not have thought directly about my mother, but I liked to take walks along the shore and look where the curve of the beach disappeared at the mist of the horizon. I liked to stand at the railing of a deck and watch the sun sink over a row of pines turning the world into gold. Okay, I *was* the sensitive one, but looking back it seems to me that I was haunted.

Now, I live in Georgia at the southern tip of Appalachian chain and still like to climb to the top of places like Blood Mountain and feel that urge to lean into the distant landscape and lose myself in the wide open vista. I read Alfred North Whitehead who says that religion is solitude and if you have never been alone you are not religious, and I thought, for a while, that divinity was found in these isolated places, but I know too, that I sought my mother there, yearned for her presence though I could never fully characterize that ache until now. She was absence, so I sought her where I could feel the piquant sting of her leaving forcibly, directly, reenacting my loss in an attempt to feel *some*thing, though, sadly, I usually felt nothing.

A lot of nothing.

~ ~ ~

During the late fall and early winter of my seventh-grade year, I would ride my bike to a deserted outdoor basketball court at Rider College near my home and spend hours dribbling and shooting and playing a game called 'do-over'. I was a scrawny kid with slow reflexes and no strong competitive instincts, and had failed to make the school team, but my best friends had, so I would spend my afternoons on the court practicing alone as if the game consisted of the high, lonely arc of shots taken from the perimeter.

On my last shot before going home, I pretended that I was at point guard in the final seconds of the game, and I had the ball. I dribbled into my favorite shooting position above the key and just off to the right of the basket, side stepped an imaginary defender, and jumped to take the shot. If I made it, I could go home the hero. The ball rolled off my fingers with my characteristically wobbly release, and seemed to float in slow motion toward the goal, rising as the sky around me turned the orange of sunset. Sometimes I did make the shot, dashed to the ball for a few short dribbles, perhaps took one more lay up for extra measure, and headed to my bike.

In retrospect, I believe that those times alone were as much about my mother as they were about basketball, this pretend game that I played happening within a year of her death. I believe that without conscious thought about her, I often reenacted the impossible to delay her final, fatal choice—a game I still play as I write this book. What mattered in my game of do-over were the times that I missed, because I never went home without making the last shot. In my mind I might claim that there was a foul at the buzzer, and I would take my place at the foul line and shoot till I made my basket keeping the unacknowledged spirit of my mother alive. Other times, weary of pretend, I just declared a "do over," over and over again till the ball at last went through the hoop and the metal chains on the basket snapped in victory and the crowd in my imaginings roared, even though I knew, by the time that I secured the ball in the rack carrier of my bike and began the slow ride home, that no basketball could fill the hollowness of the empty hoop in my life.

~ ~ ~

When I think of the years after my mother's death, I realize that I shaped who I am against the curves of her absence. That a part of me—an essential part of who I am—was, and still is, alive by contrast. Alive against the shapeliness of what isn't there. That is why I used to wonder her away—I'm pretty sure that is what I was doing—and all but the most tenacious of memories of her flickered out. I called my new step-mother "Mom" and was proud of my new older sister. This seemed like my family, a happy family, while my own mother receded as she had wished into the background. Meanwhile, the pondering, introspective side of my life deepened and thickened and grew imaginatively rich as the actual image of her faded.

One Saturday a month, during these junior high years, I would pool my allowance in order to buy an album. My dad had bought a new guitar for me, a mahogany Gibson, so I rode my bike to the University Store at Princeton to buy the latest releases from Joan Baez or Peter, Paul, & Mary. The whole trip was about fifteen miles, and took all morning, and what I remember most were the hours alone, the bike wheels whirring beneath me as I clicked through gears. I sought out these moments by myself because, I believe now, I wanted to be with her, to be in her presence. I had reached a point where I could not consciously bring myself to think of her name or see her face in my mind, but that most solitary and receptive part of me resisted in its own way the attempt that began with her and rippled through the family, to act as if she had never existed.

My favorite part of the long bike trip was the approach to Princeton where the road narrowed and the trees that lined the curbs formed a canopy overhead, and the straight stretch narrowed to a point on the horizon. My goal was to reach that point that receded ahead of me the harder I pumped my legs, and at one spot, the road began a slow decline and I could stop pumping and lean back gliding downhill, the wind tugging at my shirt and my eyes stinging in the rush of air as I lifted my hands from the handle bars to take back what had vanished from my life. If she had become her absence—no more to my life than the whisper of wind whipping past—then I would embrace that, take it in and make it my own.

~ ~ ~

When did I finally peel off her image from the scrapbook of memory and turn her into a ghost? A featureless muse? There were all of those hours playing guitar alone in my room, sublimating her, turning her from a real person into the vapor of song, the darkened sound hole of my mahogany guitar transforming the scrapings of my fingers into notes with depth and resonance. That is part of what I did to back away from her memory, I believe now, during those crucial months after her death, the guitar a surrogate for a real embrace, the resonating wood a displaced moan, the strummed sounds drifting off and away like a brunette wave.

It may have started earlier. "With all the time your mother spent in the hospital," Barbara says, "you were probably already retreating behind that wall of protection, even before your mother died." She's probably right. Even when my mother was home during that last year, I suspect that her eyes were largely vacant and staring off, as she withdrew, too. But after she died, I know I could play guitar alone, or flip a bicycle on its seat and spin the wheels, or stand and toss stones into an empty construction site for hours slowly re-enacting the loss, and, by some sort of self-hypnotic repetition of meaningless gestures, wash her memory away. *Away*, where it stayed for decades.

~ ~ ~

I'm not sure why I waited so long to read the letters or why I clung to a few melancholy images that have no story and spirited her out of time.

Knowing I couldn't change events I may have just wanted to freeze them into mental photographs that curled in on themselves. I was busy and had moved on, was a little put off by the prospect of reading about a self that I had with the help of others buried under the word "sad" long ago. I had transformed her death into a mystery, her absence into mysticism.

Sometimes I think I was afraid that the truth would strip off a protective layer of wonder from my past, replacing an airbrushed version with facts, and that knowing too much would take this secret that had for decades animated some hidden part of me, some engendering and creative aspect of who I am, and lay it bare in all of its ordinariness and tawdriness, washing the mystery out of my mother's life and mine.

Somehow I was able during those years after junior high to bracket off her death so that I could go on, live in my new family, go to college, and start a family of my own. She was not a taboo subject, not really, after I had gotten older. I could say her name and explain that she died of suicide to anyone, but I didn't feel anything when I said the words and the actual story was off limits. Any thought of what really happened felt like an intrusion. I had internalized her last wish, which was to be forgotten, so that I could live a life that was otherwise ploddingly normal.

~ ~ ~

Normal but introspective. When I was in high school, I often gazed at two paintings of gondolas in the evening by Alfred de Breanski that hung in the living room. They are companion pieces that I still like to look at when I visit my stepmother in Kentucky, each depicting a gondola floating across glassy waters toward a ship with pastel sails. They capture that time in the evening when the water and the sky are the same color, and the horizon line is reduced to a mere sequence of shadows left by the distant buildings of Venice, the details wrapped in a vague mist. My eyes work their way across the seascape past pastel sails of burnt orange, lavender, and ivory, the only bits of true color in the scene, to dark and barely discernible shapes making passage across this placid Lethe toward the luminous sails. In one painting, the gondola appears to have several figures hidden in a charcoal felze—a veiled woman, perhaps, and a man with a top hat. Behind them the gondolier leans into his oar guiding the craft. In the other painting, a lone figure stands, wending his way through calm waters, hauling two loads of fruit glowing at dusk—melons, perhaps—toward the larger ships.

My stepmother hung the paintings above a gold, brocaded sofa in the living room when we lived in New Jersey, and as a boy, I rested my arms on the sofa back and knelt in that seat, my knees in the plush, just staring at the scenes spellbound, seduced by them, getting lost in them, drifting into a shadowy place that opened like a blouse onto a creamy white.

We are "proud of our two oil paintings," my mother wrote in 1958 when she and Dad were enjoying the prosperity of his new position with the company in Chicago. "Found them in an outlet store using them for background color." In the letter she dismissed the purchase as a "conversation piece," but conversation was never an idle subject with my mother who consciously sought out props to get her through any social event. Unwilling to trust her own instincts, she had done her research. "An artist in Spring Valley says they are quite good." But something about the dreamy, otherworldly view must have caught my mother's eye in the first place since she made the choice, and, as I stand all of these years later in the living room of my stepmother's house in Paducah, looking at the paintings as an adult, I can feel the presence of my mother in her choices. She *was* proud of her purchases and luxuriated in their seductive beauty, maybe even gloating a little over their exotic, Mediterranean setting so far from the plains of Kansas and the icy northern climate of Chicago. "They show the gondolas on the water with Venice, Italy in the background," she wrote, a hint of self-satisfaction in her cosmopolitan taste, but I know that she also felt drawn to these scenes of water and sky with shadows at the edges and at the core because I feel it too, this picture that she chose having seduced me long ago and shaped my aesthetic.

It is not the figures on the gondolas that held her eye and hold mine now but the interiors of the ships they are heading toward, the insides of their hulls varicolored, almost like the dark half of an artist's palette, thick with paint suggesting huddled bodies hidden in the textures beneath the backdrop of canvas sails. These shapes draw me in further—they always did, even when I was a boy—because this painting taught me how to see them as she did, the half-lit figures gargoylish and sinister, flanking the sickle-shaped rudder, a Dantean scene of passage to a netherworld that my mother knew well and tried to protect me from, a blackness that must have registered with her when she first walked up to the painting hanging among others in the outlet store, and as I gaze now I sense her standing beside me, leaning in, and feel her shiver of recognition as the figures on the boat gaze back blankly.

"That is what she gave you," Barbara said one morning when I was trying to figure out the importance of art in my mother's letters. I had just trudged upstairs after several frustrating hours at the writing desk, leaving my pile of scattered pages behind, and we were having coffee as usual on the sofa. "This is what you share." It is true. I too feel the tug of such scenes, the pull of the open, darkening sky illuminated here and there by remnants of light. I seek out those places as a refuge, just as she did.

~ ~ ~

Many years ago, my boys and I hiked up Blood Mountain that looms above the Dahlonega Plateau in

Georgia, one of the last great peaks at the southern tip of the Appalachian chain where mountains give way to the wide, flat expanse of coastal plains. I loved to watch Sam chase Matt up the switchback paths at the beginning of the trip, both boys laughing out loud while I trudged behind. We came to an overlook, about halfway to the top, a slab of rock cantilevered into the open skies high above the valley, and when I walked to the edge of the stone ledge, I had to check a foolish impulse to fly. Crows floated below me, and a small Cessna buzzed into the distance at eye level. A hawk cut a lazy circle overhead, dragging a flittering shadow across the treetops at my feet. Fly—yes, it looked so easy.

I saw the universe spread before me, not just mountains and streams and a blanket of trees, but the whole mighty thing, and even when I reached my hand out tentatively to break the plane of this apparition of infinite depth, I could not put the vision in perspective. The lesser hills seemed to emanate from me, the topography of the land wrenched into submission like a supplicant at my feet by a grand *trompe l'oiel*, even though I knew that the view was not created for my eye. I was created for it. I put my hand to my eyes, surveying a blue that looked pristine simply because it hung above a horizon line that was so far away, and saw a rough blanket of treetops a half mile below spread in lumpy folds across a darkening expanse to a misty horizon, promising me a safe landing somewhere in Tennessee. It was a variation of the gondola scene with a misty horizon, a spreading darkness, and me standing at a precipice gliding forward, drawn by the power of the panorama and buoyed by an unearthly feeling of calm—or, perhaps, a sadness so perpetual that it came masked as calm. A sense of being beyond it all where your personal feelings do not go away but do not matter. A kind of wonder. I stood at the bow of my life, transfixed, and the urge to spread my arms, lean into that emptiness, and yield to infinity was hard to resist.

Just a step, I thought perched on the rocky outcropping at the edge of forever. It would be easy.

I held my breath and closed my eyes. Oh, yes. I *want* this.

Only when my son shouted, "Hey Dad, it's over here," his voice the call of the familiar directing me to the main path, to him and his brother and life, did I step back bewildered, and, reluctantly, turn away.

~ ~ ~

When I was a boy, I liked to kneel in the sticks and gravel and leaves strewn about the woods behind our house in Nanuet, and crack open rocks. While the voices of friends playing marbles or baseball up by the road receded from my attention, I held a stone in hand, took a breath, lifted my Dad's ball peen hammer, and, as time stopped, focused my mind on the unbroken stone which hid its glory under a dusty, plain, pitted exterior. Often when the hammer head came down it would open up a fossilized scene from a primordial past and set my niche in the planet beyond time and place.

There in my hands, chips of stone fell away from petrified gastropods, brachiopods, and trilobites, the calcified remains of corkscrew-shaped creatures from a time millions of years earlier. When I dropped the hammer and held my fossil treasure up close, running my fingertips over the preserved scroll patterns in the rock, the veiled grove protected me, hemming me in like the mist of a Venetian evening. Now I know that when I was cracking open these stony wonders, my mother was watching from the porch, and writing letters, the scattered pages of our story forming under her hands. I suspect, too, that she understood why I retreated to this place. It called to me, this natural opening formed by an arched canopy of twisted limbs that led to a dark path in the woods, but now I know because she often watched me from the back porch, that it called to the her in me, as it does still when I look into the opening in the tangle of trees and shrubs that leads to the source of the stream behind my house in Georgia.

In 1956 my mother mentions how hectic life can be with an outgoing husband and two young boys. She called it the "low roar" of family life, Dad arranging parties and hunting excursions and business trips and my brother and I tumbling about rambunctiously. In the letter she complains that she had to interrupt her writing because Ron had just "dashed" up to her in desperate need of war gear. "I had to stop and cut out a cardboard feather and sword so that he could be Robin Hood." My dad was slated for a trip to Chicago the next day and she mentions that she is "almost glad to see him go," though she adds her ambiguous "ha" in parentheses and admits she actually enjoys the commotion. "No, I really like it," she explains, "but I also need quiet times, or days, too."

It is the phrase "or days" that hits me, the longing for an extended period of silence to pull herself together and begin at last that slow ride to the dark hull that called to her, to us. Somewhere in the making of her story, I realized that this book was not only about her absence which shaped me, but also her presence in me, giving voice at last to a collaboration where the part of me that sought her all those years met the part of her that she had long ago left behind. Two halves of the same longing.

~ ~ ~

Wonder Question: What is it that seems to talk to me when the world is dark and still?

"What does the world mean? And why am I here? Where are all the people who have been and gone? Where does the rose come from? Who holds the stars up? What is it that seems to talk to me when the world is dark and still?" These are the wonder questions that Marjorie Mee asked her mother, and lately I've been thinking about the last one. When "the world" goes away who speaks to me? For my mother, "the world" was the in-fighting at American Cyanamid, the Dave Garroway show in the morning, and the Estes Keefauver hearings at night, her energetic and likable husband, the melancholy moan of Peggy Lee, her house which was a familiar foe, her parents, my grandmother who actually talked back and my grandfather who communicated with her on a level beyond words, my brother who brought joy and his eyes which complicated her nightmare. It included her many fears and anxieties. And of course it included me. *The Book of Knowledge* was her crib sheet on this world, "a book that will answer all the questions," Marjorie's mother exclaimed, a weapon and a crutch hidden in plain sight in the middle of the family room.

But what did my mother hear when she closed the book? When she put us to bed and turned off the TV and record console on those long nights when my father was away, the "quiet times" she said she needed? I linger over the phrase "dark and still" in my wonder question. Mornings were her hard time, but she loved the dusk: the glowing fire of an evening picnic at the side of a Kansas highway, the darkening horizon at sunset after long rides on Cricket in the open prairie around Dodge, the Hudson River Valley at the end of a long day, the water glassy smooth and lit by a glowing moon, and the scene, dark and still, of shapes fading into the mists of the Venetian lagoon. She would have welcomed a gravesite swept clean by the winds and rains and blanching sun of the Kansas prairie. She knew about the beauty of what is passing and the shapeliness of what isn't there, and for most of my life, I grudgingly acknowledged the motive of her last, gloomy achievement. If I had not read the letters, I suspect that I would have been content with that awful and final gratuity, tossed casually beside the unpaid bill.

But I did read her letters, sitting in the armchair in my den in Georgia, and on one chilly November morning I paused in my reading, looked at late autumn sunlight pouring through the bay window, and saw a vision that gave my mother back to me. I saw envelopes, swept up in a tiny whirlwind in my mind, forming a mobile before me. The haphazard scattering of stationery, whipped into a spiral by the imagination and animated by loss, composed itself into an orbiting shape of beauty and power that mesmerized me then and that I can see even now if I close my eyes, a momentary vision that was never far from my thoughts as I kept reading.

I began checking out books about the artist Alexander Calder, the creator of the mobile, from the library and ordered some online. More books to share the shelves with *The Books of Knowledge*. I found Calder's remarkably happy and straightforward *Autobiography*, the massive *Alexander Calder 1898-1976* full of enormous color photographs of his work, and a slim volume, edited by Calder's grandson, Alexander S. C. Rower, called *Caldersculpture*. My friend, the artist Dick Aunspaugh, loaned me his copy of *Calder's Universe*, the best book on the artist. I checked out the website sponsored by the

Calder Foundation and found other images of his work online at the sites of various museums and collectors, including some video clips of the mobiles in motion.

At night, when I grew tired of reading the letters, I would walk down to my study and pull the oversized volumes of Calder down from the makeshift shelf I had set up on a bureau. I liked to leaf through the heavy, glossy pages, running my hands over the plates of mobiles, and taking in their odd and intriguing names: *Red Gongs, Floating Wood Objects and Wire Spines, Hanging Spider, Polygones Noirs, Dots and Dashes, Five Red Arcs, .127,* and *Elements Démontables.* I noticed the sweep of far-flung ovals, oblongs, and wings in these constructions suspended in air at the edge of emptiness and the smaller orbits of the inner circle of lesser disks, and inevitably my eye fell to that locus where the central wire met the main rod, the "point of support" Calder called it, a phrase that registers on the mind as a term from engineering, but falls from the lips with alliterative playfulness, like the mouth spitting out pins. "Point of support." Who *does* hold the stars up? What message did that crossing of rods tucked in at the still center of a mobile have to tell me? Why did my mother's letters lead me there?

~ ~ ~

I searched for the answer in the artist's biography. At the age of twenty-three, Alexander Calder acquired a seaman's ticket and a job with the crew of the *H. F. Alexander* for a one-way voyage from New York to Hawaii and San Francisco via the Panama Canal. He worked in the boiler room, grimy work. It got so hot that he rigged up a baffle to direct cool air toward him while he watched and loaded the boiler. When he took a break, Calder, like the rest of the crew, often slept on the piles of rolled up hawser on deck. There he had an epiphany:

175

It was early one morning on a calm sea, off Guatemala, when over my couch—a coil of rope—I saw the beginning of a fiery sunrise on one side and the moon looking like a silver coin on the other. Of the whole trip this impressed me most of all; it left me with a lasting impression of the solar system.

In Calder's moment, the details matter—the fiery sunrise, the moon like a silver coin, and the rope. They glide through the warm morning of his vision like the three Graces. He has not yet created his first mobile, but it is all there, the orb of day on one side with the orb of night on the other, the fiery "and" and the silvery "and yet." In that auroral moment the solar system presented itself to the artist as a mobile of radiant objects looped together in perfect suspension by invisible gravitational forces and bound to him at the point of support by a coil of rope, and even though he did not understand his vision at first, he felt the truth of a lifetime implicit in his sense of celestial objects in equilibrium slowly orbiting in space. I think of the boy and girl on the frontispiece of *The Children's Encyclopædia* standing at the margin of the page and pointing into a whirl of planetary spheres, streaking comets, backlit clouds, glowing stars, a crescent moon, and a sun surrounded by a nimbus.

~   ~   ~

Not content with the books, I found myself drawn to look at Calder's work, needing to see the mobiles themselves, and took the trip with Barbara to the National Gallery in Washington D. C. to walk through the extensive exhibit there. When we entered the building, she walked up to the concierge desk to ask a question while I, wonderstruck, meandered under the enormous black and blue wings and red petals of a huge mobile that floated several stories above me. "The *Aluminum Honeycomb*," I said when she joined me and we wandered into the enormous gallery. We decided to go our separate ways, so Barbara followed the underground corridor to the main building next door leaving me alone to explore Calder's work in the East Gallery.

I wandered into a white-walled room on the bottom floor devoted to the artist, a room filled with color, shadows, and slowly spinning shapes. I sat down on the floor. From here I had a perfect view of *Black and White and Ten Red*, a mobile he built in 1957, the year of Sputnik when my family moved to Deerfield. I made notes.

> Two equal ovals—one black and one white—on separate stems, fan out in opposite directions. Below them, ten red petals are strewn on the air, spilling in a wild array beyond the boundary marked off by the orbit of the black and white shapes. What contraries are these? Shape and shadow, night and day, sun and moon, man and woman? And what of the crimson progeny that dangle below the pair?

Of all the mobiles in this room, this one had the most dramatic movement. Suspended by a long thin wire from a hook in the ceiling, it rode currents of air, slowly gyrating back and forth like a sleepy weathervane. Dents running in a small crescent along the surface of the white oval gave it a cratered and pocked look. Did Calder take a hammer to it? In frustration? In anger? Or did he find it that way? Was damage built into this mobile, or was it found to be in the nature of the materials before he started?

177

The white disc bears the secret like a scar. The black disc has no secrets. It is a purer object, all emptiness, a wide hole of velvety oblivion as I view it face on, thinning to a single black line as the mobile turns. They are the full moon and the new, these contrary disks, waxing and waning in tandem above sublunary puddles of blood.

I lowered my pencil and gazed for a long time at the structure oscillating in front of me. Parts in isolation do not define a mobile. It is the relationship among the parts and the space that the parts move through that matter, and the relationships constantly change which matters as well. Frozen in words, the mobile is an abstract tableau of good and evil with a finite number of consequences. It doesn't hold still and that is its dreamy truth, but it doesn't float randomly either. When it reached the end of a counter-clockwise spin, the mobile paused briefly, and my thoughts wound through and around the structure like a slow stroll in moonlight, until the dangling contraption nudged itself awake and began the retrograde rotation, continually reinventing itself.

I thought of an angelfish suspended in a tank full of predators.

~ ~ ~

"The shadows," one young woman said upon entering the room. "So awesome." I was sitting on the floor, making more notes and she did not see me. Stylish and pretty, she wore a navy jumper with a white blouse and tapped a brochure impatiently against her palm as she glanced around at the mobiles draped everywhere. She turned, looked at her friend who shrugged, and they both walked off, leaving me alone again.

178

She's right, I realized, looking anew at the room with its high ceiling and nooks illuminated by recessed lights, all filled with Calder's spinning art. The shadows do change everything. Without them, the room is a kindergarten. All here and now, the mobiles giddy in their colors. But the shadows, like gathering clouds, are a pensive presence you hardly notice at first, the flat replicas that hover in various shades of gray about each innocent object. Lit from below, the mobiles cast feathery bruises on the high walls overhead, the contours distorted as they reach for the ceiling and contorted as they overlap, shuffling ghosts, some dark and precise, others faded and smudgy. They lurk about, ministerial and attentive, deferential even, keenly aware of the slightest movement of the mobile itself which they mimic while whispering conspiratorially.

~ ~ ~

I returned to the atrium of the museum to take a last look at the *Aluminum Honeycomb* mobile this time from above the two-story opening at the East Gallery entrance. I saw a sweep of dark wings, some with boomerang shapes and others more like the cocked back silhouettes of stealth bombers, arc momentarily, metallic swifts in flight, and follow each other down and away, wingtips tilting in currents of air, most of them jet black, though the last in the u-shape of wings has a gun-metal blue cast. Wild, menacing, skittish—those are the words that came to mind. Looking at the sculpture, I thought of darts and bats and blown debris. I thought of bullets fanned out on a car seat.

At the opposite end of the structure hung six large petals painted bright red. Suspended from five stems, the rounded shapes drooped below the pitched wings, the last one floating above the pointing fingers of children passing below. These carmine ovals appeared to drift out of reach, the smallest petal dangling at the greatest distance, with some of the red shapes cupped and others flat creating the illusion of casual disarray that we find in falling leaves. I thought of kites and bows and bright red buttons. I thought of medium velocity blood spatter.

"A mobile," Jean-Paul Sartre wrote in a catalog for an Alexander Calder exposition in Paris in 1946, is composed of "pure and changing forms, at once so free and so disciplined," and the Aluminum Honeycomb does appear to vault free of its center like an acrobat poised in air. Suspended above the two-story opening at the gallery entrance it stretches seventy-six feet across the sunlit room and dangles just above the border of the cut-away floor, spilling over the walkway itself, suggesting excitement and danger, an explosion of forms that will not be contained. It crisscrosses in silhouette the grid of geodesic girders in the skylight overhead with a dizzying disregard of symmetry.

And yet—because with Calder there is always this "and yet"—the arrangement is stable, harmonious, and equiponderant, all of its parts chastened by gravity and disciplined at its point of support. This is not a flight of fancy or confetti tossed in the air or balloons released on the winds amid a sky of changing shapes. It is only an "apparent accident" as Calder was fond of saying, because, I thought, stepping back to take it all in, the entire unwieldy contraption dangles from a single, still spot at the point where knowledge yields to wonder.

~ ~ ~

The word that matters is "apparent," right? An *apparent* accident. The artist mistakes a shape and shapes a mistake. When did the accident of the wedding become apparent? The accident of my brother's eyes? The accident of me? The objects and colors appear to have been tossed into the air on a whim. Like currents of jazz improvisation. Or the burst of seedpods along a trail. Or the spray of a horse's mane. Like a box pattern on a sofa. Or the bobbing heads of pansies. Or tropical fish floating through a cloud of bubbles. Like random nails hammered into a riser or bullets spread out on the front seat of a car or the spatter of blood on asphalt. "No human brain, not even their creator's, could possibly foresee all the complex combinations of which they are capable," Sartre wrote in a description of Calder's mobiles. "A general destiny of movement is sketched out for them, and they are left to work it out for themselves." Objects in a mobile come in different sizes and shapes, wires can vary in length, and the point of balance is rarely found at the center of each rod, bestowing on the whole higgledy-piggledy contraption a semblance of the haphazard, but, appearances aside, it always dangles from a single point: hidden, but fixed; revealed, not created; felt, not known.

~ ~ ~

Once Sartre's described a mobile that had started rotating after a long period of quiescence. "It began mournfully to wave." So I was disappointed that the *Aluminum Honeycomb* did not move. I had read that it picks up the currents created by heating vents and slowly turns, but even on this cold day in February when the heat was on in the East Gallery, the construction didn't budge. Eventually, I asked the docent if it always hangs perfectly still this way. He looked surprised and walked close. "No sir,' he said turning toward the huge mobile and winding his finger slowly. "Some days it turns. It goes slowly, but, yes sir," he said looking up at the structure frozen now in place and extending across the atrium, dangling from its point of support. "It goes round."

It was then that I saw a boy looking up as he walked with his mother downstairs under the *Aluminum Honeycomb,* and I began to understand at last what had drawn me here. Without taking his eyes off of the mobile, the boy let go of his mother's hand and his body slowly turned, obeying some internal gravitational tug of the object of his curiosity, and the mother in jeans paused with him, but, as I recreate the scene in my mind now, she wears a swing dress with pearl, clip-on earrings and a pill box hat, and, when she bends down beside her son saying something in his ear, her Gimbles' shopping bag tips over. The boy, in sneakers and a t-shirt, may have stood in wonder as the mobile floated above, but in my imagination he sports a bow tie and a high, blond wave. After a moment, his mother checks her watch and stands adjusting her floral skirt. Time to go. She and the boy hurry on together into the museum, though he casts one last glance up—this time at me.

~ ~ ~

"I only feel elation if I've got ahold of something good," Calder explained in a conversation with Selden Rodman published in *Calder's Universe.* "I start by cutting lots of shapes. Next, I file them and smooth them off." Some of the parts he chose because they were "pleasing or dynamic" and others he found by chance. Then he arranged them on a flat surface putting the wire supports between the pieces and making additional cuts with shears, "calculating for balance this time." It is all "cut and try" he told a reporter from *Look* magazine. When he was asked how he decided on the counterweights for each part of the design, he said that he let the materials guide him:

I begin with the smallest and work up. Once I know the balance point for this first pair of discs, I anchor it by a hook to another arm, where it acts as one end of another pair of scales, and so on up. It's a kind of ascending scale of weights and counterweights.

Amid a whirl of shapes the artist feels his way along a wire to that point of support which is a product of the abundance and order of a universe for the moment subject to his will. "You put a disc here and then you put another disc there," Calder explained, "then you balance them on your finger and keep adding."

Returning home from the Calder exhibit in Washington, I fumbled through the boxes of my mother's letters, arranging them, spreading them out on the felt of the pool table in my basement den among the pictures and memorabilia from the wicker basket before I started writing. "Begin with the smallest and then work up." Follow the "ascending scale of weights and counterweights" and "balance them on your finger and keep adding" until you find the "point of support," the "point of stillness," I thought, excited now about the idea of writing about my mother as a way to feel her again in my life. I would get lost along the way, I knew, distracted by the dailiness of each letter written for a certain set of the week's occasions and filled with the twiggy twists and turns of the here and now. My book would be a kind of gathering, an anthology of her days and, eventually, our days, and any sense of the whole would have to emerge slowly as the seemingly endless mornings and afternoons piled up. Some subjects would swell out of proportion and I would be knocked off course by awful discoveries that would shake the larger whole, but over time each of these outsized moments, even the one that took place in a park in a Chicago suburb on a spring morning in April

1961, would be subsumed within the larger story, which is not her story but our story. That, I realized at last, was my task: to assemble it all and fashion a whole, bringing these boxes of her words to my few, faulty memories and grainy photographic images in search of clues to the hidden tale with the wonder questions from *The Book of Knowledge* as my guide. I would drape a mobile of words from a hook in our universe where knowledge and wonder meet and watch the unfolding of the "general destiny of movement" that had been "sketched out" for us.

As I gazed at the letters spread before me, an apparent accident slowly turned my way.

In March 2012, after I had written most of my book, Barbara and I went back to Deerfield. It was the first time I had been back since the death of my mother when I was eleven. We stayed at the Palmer House, the grand hotel in downtown Chicago where my dad would entertain guests for American Cyanamid and where he and my mother celebrated his promotion to District Manager. I sat in the large, leather chairs in The Empire Room early on our first morning while Barbara slept. I took off my watch to set the date—this was the first day of March in a leap year—and heard a sultry jazz vocal piped into the room with the refrain line "time passing by" repeated over and over. I had made a few arrangements for our room at the front desk earlier and the clerk had asked about my stay so far. I said, incongruously, that my parents used to come to this hotel years ago. "When I was a boy," I added, somehow proud of the fact.

There is no presence of them here now, I think, as I look around at men in ball caps and sweatshirts and women in sneakers, all checking their cell phones. A different world. A different time. "Time passing by." And yet, when I look up at the ornate clock held by naked deities above the entrance to the lobby, the rococo ceiling border with its Wedgwood-like scenes of white marble embossed on alternating blue and green panels and held in place by gold-tipped Corinthian columns, or when I lean back to take in the enormous ceiling painting of figures from Greek myth with a naked Venus walking on water as the centerpiece, her hair blown back in Botticellian disarray as her body emerges from a flowing gown, the folds falling into a stylized column behind her, or when I level my gaze on the red-carpeted marble stairway that spills into the room with torch-like finials on either side held up by newel posts of Emperador-marble figurines—when I look at all of this, I know that The Empire Room is a conscious attempt to resist time's passing, and whether all of this gaudiness succeeds or not, I look ahead and see the image of my mother emerge from the marble stairway in a smart pencil dress with wide lapels, a feminine presence—not maternal, not here in this hotel lobby—glancing around the room in search of someone, probably Dad and "the boys" from Cyanamid who will meet her for cocktails on a night some fifty years ago before heading out to Chez Paree. She glances at the clock, checking the "time passing by" and pauses a moment looking about, before descending the stairs, sitting in one of the divans, like the one across from me now, settling her cocktail purse, crossing her legs seductively, and looking right through me.

Later, Barbara and I head out to Deerfield by train, crossing the flat Illinois landscape in winter under a solid gray sky. It is cold when we arrive at the station on a slope that sits above the town. While we put on our coats and gloves, we looked down on Jewett Park from the station, a ball field where I played little-league games. It is a wide green with an arena of some sort in the back, the grounds bounded by hardwoods and a few pines. When she dropped Dad off at the station that April morning in 1961 did she drive through this park? When did she buy the gun? Where? Questions, yes, but not wonder questions. We see the flashing lights of a patrol car pulling someone over, and I think of the suspicious policeman following my mother that day. Nothing suspicious now. The park looks calm under an implacable sky, more like a photograph than a story. It will keep its secrets.

Pulling our coats tight, Barbara and I walk the short distance across town toward Warrington Road. Much of Deerfield has built up since my mother died and the family moved away, but when we get past the new shopping center with a Starbucks and a Barnes and Noble, I see the church on the corner and know I'm home.

"I sang a solo once in the choir there," I say to Barbara.

"Nice," she says as we pause, looking at the plain brick building with a white steeple. "Methodist."

We move on approaching an old and established house, the former construction site where my little ten-year-old girlfriend followed me while I walked wooden planks over mud gathering slugs as if they were treasure. I smile at the memory.

We turn down my street.

"I used to sing at night walking home here after choir practice," I said, remembering for a moment how bright the stars could be at night there glittering in the cold, and the smoke of my breath as I sang hymns to fill the darkness. When we turn the corner, I point to a brick house behind ours. "There is the yard they flooded each winter for a skating rink."

We passed the Tudor style house that belonged to the Robinson's, and I pointed out the two upper story windows facing each other where Jamie and I strung our telephone made of paper cups and twine. At last we arrive at our house.

For a while we look in silence at the small split-level with a picture window that faces the street. An enormous tree, low to the ground but with a wide, rounded crown, dominates the center of the yard. It's winter so I can't tell what kind of tree it is, but it was not here when we lived in the house. Peering past the branches, I see the steps where my mother caught Chris and me looking at a *Playboy*, and the line of hedges that Chris had to go through when he was sent back to his place. I lead Barbara to the side yard and point to the corner of the back of the garage. "My mother and I planted pansies there," I say, pointing to a margin of exposed earth that lines the garage. "That bed goes around behind the house."

Not much to see, really. We return to the front of the house again, and I try to look into the picture window, but from the sidewalk I cannot make out much.

"I think the steps came down here," I say pointing to the left side of the window. "I remember my dad coming down those stairs, suitcases banging. I think it was on that side of the room."

"Probably was," Barbara says, leaning forward to see better, checking out the layout. "Yes, probably."

"It ended in a landing at the door."

She looks again, nodding.

"I remember Dad coming down the steps, and on this side"—I point to the other end of the picture window—"I see my grandparents sitting."

I look harder, but the dark window yields nothing. As usual, I cannot picture my mother. "What I remember may be from that day," I tell Barbara, referring to my mother's suicide. "I just can't be sure."

Barbara nods and lets me look for a while longer.

The story is not here, I realize, studying the house that is both familiar and strange. My mother stared out of that picture window as she listened to music, rushed out of this door to keep her boy from breaking a neighbor's window once, and put her fingers in the soil of the garden at the back of the house when she and I planted pansies together. She walked these hardwood floors, I wrote later, while jotting notes in the Deerfield train station built in 1907, and she probably sat on these hard wooden benches, dressed up and ready for a rendezvous at The Palmer House, looking out on the bungalows just beyond the tracks as I am doing now. Notebook in hand, I leave Barbara for a moment and walk to the other side of the station for one last look at the park where winter trees reach up forming a thorny ring. Somewhere near here my mother wrapped her index finger around the trigger of a forty-four caliber pistol, looked into that raw wilderness, and squeezed. All that is true, I think, closing my notebook and walking back to sit by Barbara, but she is not here now and her story is not here either.

It is in me.

~ ~ ~

There are other legacies of my mother and the family that nurtured her that are more revealing of who she was than our old neighborhood in the town that shows no sign of her presence and the train station beside the tracks that lead to nowhere. I have inherited more than her ghost floating down the marble stairway at The Palmer House, taking her place among the figurines that stare off at nothing. On our bed at home in Georgia, Barbara and I have a quilt made by my grandmother's sewing circle out of squares fashioned from my mother's childhood dresses. The patches from the dresses are pastel flower designs sewn into squares and assembled on a large frame by the hands of my grandmother's friends. When I shake it open, the quilted colors billow overhead and ride the air down, like folds in the dress of a dancing child, the quilt settling playfully on the bedspread, its colored patches unfurled in a loosely symmetrical design. I'm no expert, but I can tell as I run my fingers over the cloth, that the hand stitching is intricate and tight. Barbara and my daughter Alice, who also quilts, agree. When I flip the quilt over on itself and examine the back stitches—the top design in reverse—the handwork is equally striking, carving out a web of nearly identical snowflake patterns repeating endlessly in the folds on the side where the colors of my mother's dresses seem to have washed away.

The legacy of fine craftsmanship in our family goes back even further. A stately, walnut secretary that my great, great grandfather made with simple hand tools some time near the end of the nineteenth century stands in the corner of our living room like a lonely sentinel on the past. The cabinet rises nearly eight feet from the floor and the bold vertical lines are crowned with a molded cornice. No ornament in the cabinet draws attention to itself. The hand-carved arrow accent piece in the crown, repeated in the side pilasters and in the base, is subtle and greets the eye only as it comes to the hand. As I look at it, I find my fingers drawn to the honey surfaces that my ancestor varnished and rubbed smooth, and I see the glow of my features reflected in its depths.

The tall top shelf, laden though it is with photographs of our family, looks light and airy. It and the other shelves—closer together and crammed with more photographs as well as old books, wire-rimmed spectacles, and other knickknacks—are given over to sentiment. These shelves speak to the past in hushed tones while the desk below is all business, a maze of wooden drawers, tiny shelves, and tall vertical file dividers constructed of wood. Here papers—clipped, rolled, stacked and jammed-in every which-way—declare the secretary's utilitarian *raison d'etre*, the felt-covered desktop hidden under formidable documents announcing pressing matters, though on Easter these cubbies and corners also shed their worldly ways and have in the past been transformed into preferred hiding places for brightly-colored eggs.

The secretary was built in Pella, Iowa, but how it got from Iowa to my grandparents' home near the Solomon River in Kansas, where I first saw it, remains a mystery. It may have missed the first trip into the territory when my great, great grandfather, Don Peaslee, and his wife Elizabeth made the move in June of 1870. It is not mentioned in Elizabeth's memoir of the time and since she does make a list of the belongings they carried, the omission of the secretary seems conclusive. As I look at it rising toward the ceiling in my living room I have trouble even imagining that it could make the covered wagon trip across the prairie. No doubt, an eight-foot secretary, even one that breaks down into parts, would have increased the load and made crossing of "the raging torrent" of rivers like Coon Creek and The Republican hazardous. But my grandmother always insisted that the secretary made the first trip, and, since it belonged to her grandfather, she was certainly closer to the truth than anyone else I know.

Somehow it got to Kansas and survived. My grandparents refinished the piece, sanding clean the old lacquer "all one winter," my grandmother wrote, and applying new varnish by hand. Today my hand rests on the scrolled pilaster, and the faces of my children, at many ages of their lives, crowd the shelves. Preserved for six generations by utility and beauty, Don Peaslee's secretary has come to own a corner of our house by the force of its simple lines, beautiful finish, and family history.

No one knows where Don Peaslee learned carpentry, but Elizabeth, his wife, whose maiden name was Smith, comes from a long line of craftsmen who trace their lineage back through the founder of the family in

191

America, Captain John Smith, to Hamo de Carington, the friend and "Armor Smith" of William the Conqueror. According to a family history called *The Smiths and the Chamberlains*, the smithy "made the shields, swords, spearheads and arrow tips" for the army that William had assembled at Hastings nearly a thousand years ago in 1066, and "being of an artistic temperament he put certain designs on the shields to identify them." I think of Don Peaslee chiseling perfect notches out of walnut and the power and care behind the blades that dug into the delicate curves of the glass doors.

Like my children, my mother played in the room that held this secretary, and associated it with home, and it is this binding of us, my mother and me, within a larger family that I see emerge when I look at it. When she saw one like it at an antique museum in New York in the fifties, she thought of Kansas and the family farm outside of Glen Elder. It "brought back many happy memories," the secretary symbolizing family for her, not simply the tight insulated family she knew as an only child, but a larger sense of family that begins somewhere in medieval France and winds through the Iowa town of Pella on its way across Coon Creek and The Republican River to Glen Elder, Kansas.

I have, in time, learned to love these gifts—this legacy of familiar things—and, since they endured the journey back east to our house in Georgia after my grandmother died, I have made them my own. The quilt has frayed at the edges, and one square is torn where I caught my toe on it one night while dreaming, and, despite its strength and beauty, collapse has been hammered into the walnut secretary that was built to last. Somewhere between the time that my great, great grandfather wiped his hands with a cloth and stepped back from his finished cabinet and the summer that my grandfather refinished the entire piece, a hinge ripped loose from one of the glass doors taking a strip of wood with it, and the hinge had to be relocated a little further down the frame because of the damaged wood. But the cabinet is still here, a bit tattered, but lovely and dignified, a reminder along with the bedspread that the story of my mother, brother, and me is the torn corner of a larger family quilt going back in history.

~ ~ ~

It extends into the future, as well. While I was writing this book my youngest daughter lived with us during a temporary hiatus between her years in Ecuador as a Peace Corps volunteer and graduate school in Atlanta. At twenty-six, Alice is in her youthful prime with long, dark hair and soft hazel eyes. We call her Smudge sometimes because of her olive complexion. She doesn't really look like either Barbara or me and does not have the blond coloring of her brothers and sister. One evening after dinner I told her that I thought she looked very much like my mother. I asked her to come downstairs to my study to look at a photo—*the* photo of my mother with Ron and me on the sofa. Alice took the frame in her long and slender fingers to get a better look, and I watched her examining the picture, her body lean and athletic from swimming and yoga, studying the image with her dark eyes, cocking one eyebrow.

Alice has the same dark hair and skin tone as my mother. Like her, her eyebrows are clearly defined and lift high, naturally, over the brow ridge. The two of them share a high forehead, wide-set eyes, and darkened eye-sockets. Like my mother, Alice has a thin nose, bobbed chin, and, though they are both feminine, my mother and Alice hold themselves in a lanky, slightly Tomboyish way. What separates them, of course, is Alice's disposition which is sunny and confident and outgoing, but in looks, they are dead ringers.

"I think you're right," she said, looking at me and smiling, before looking back at the picture again.

~ ~ ~

Barbara and I cannot remember for sure how the quilts, handcrafted furniture and wicker basket of pictures came into our possession. We had recently built the house that we have lived in for more than a quarter century and had four children at home when the stuff arrived so it was a busy time, but we think that this family legacy came to us about the same time as the letters. My mother would not have thought of the letters as falling into the category of family heirlooms, and she would not have considered them to be finely crafted, but they are. She was overly fond of the word "gorgeous" as she knew, but in many of the letters I hear the voice of thought, composed with care and cobbled into place without fuss in a language that sounds so like speech that none of the seams show. They are my mother's quilt of colored squares, her hand-crafted cabinet of dark nooks and secret drawers. Every one of them bristles with detail and, in some, the details are composed in a way that is lilting and lyrical.

"We took our first drive yesterday," she wrote on Monday, November 20, 1950 from a brick bungalow in Monsey, New York when she and Dad first moved away from Kansas to live in the northeast. I was less than two years old. "We took the Hudson River Drive on the way up," she explains. "The scenery around here is gorgeous." She mentions that she is sending pictures, and I find the colored postcards in my wicker box, stiff and pretty colorized photographs of West Point and the river, but her words say more than the pictures. "The river is very large, calm, and beautiful," she writes. Having lived in the prairie all of her life she is unaccustomed to seeing large bodies of water and is filled with wonder. "Saw the ships and were quite thrilled—first large ones I've ever seen. We took Bear Mountain Drive home. We were sorry we didn't get to see all of this because it got dark before we got home. It is completely dark by five here."

My mother weathered the mental cyclone of depression much of her adult life and that is certainly her story, but there are moments when she paints, in words, another self, whole and wonder-struck, and the whirlwind of her paranoia stops. These small epiphanies often happen outdoors or while looking outdoors, and record a joyous embrace of a wide and open sky. They are sublime glimpses of grandeur, often bounded by darkness—the blackness that finally claimed her, creeping in at the edges—but they are also marked by a brilliance of light and an expansive vista that is exhilarating. The sights transported her, lifted her momentarily out of the troubles of life; they helped her to be her best self and re-engage with family.

"The river was calm as glass and the moon was almost full," she wrote about the Hudson on a different trip with Dad and their friends Bill and Ginger Johnson, five years later. "And with the gorgeous scenery along the Hudson at dusk it was breathtakingly beautiful. And the night was more so."

She describes a flight back from Kansas in prose reminiscent of her descriptions of seeing the Hudson River. "Had such a smooth flight from K.C. to N.Y. Slept part of the way. The plane was very crowded when we boarded so I had to sit on the inside seat of the three [seat] row which was fine except I couldn't see out too well but thought the views of K.C. and Chicago were gorgeous. Looked like a huge Christmas display." She explains that she arrived early in LaGuardia and took the time to freshen up before meeting us. "When I walked out I saw Max & boys—called to them. The boys were so surprised for a second—I squatted on my knees—Ronnie said, 'Mommy' and gave me a big hug. I hugged Steve with my other arm. He put his arms around my neck and said 'Hello, Mommy.'"

After my mother died I forgot the sensation of her touch and the sound of her voice. I could not hug a shadow. I could not fill her silence with my words.

Who is suicide? She was suicide.

She became her death.

And the pictures, hundreds of curled shavings of the past in a basket, did not bring her back. Even when my mother gazed directly into the camera, I knew that she was looking into a future that was already over with shadows like gun smoke folded into the glossy black-and-white. I needed a voice, speaking in her present, not one whispering to posterity, a voice animated by the desire to capture the present for someone alive. *That* is the voice I heard in the letters. When I read them, I got to know her—for the first time, really—know her and miss her. Miss *her*, not some made up idea of her. The letters do not bring her back—I know the loss is permanent and irrevocable—but while I read them the pain, that had been nothing more than a dull throb, changed in character, becoming softer, more diffuse, and ardent, like heartache.

"They each held on to my hands," my mother wrote describing our triumphal exit from the polished rotunda at LaGuardia airport. "They kept talking to me about how happy they were that I was home—and sorta beamed."

~ ~ ~

Wonder Question: Why am I here?

196

So we have undertaken this task together, my mother and I, composing our story. Mother creating son to meet her needs, son creating mother to…no, that's too neat a formulation. I need to be precise as I come to the end of this book of gnawing and awe. The letters arrived in an entourage of familiar things as an antidote to the silence that had been my past, and though I did not listen for many years, they eventually insisted that I learn who my mother was so that I could begin to understand who I am. But they did more than that. They placed a chisel and awl in my hand and a quilter's needle in my fingertips, and when I read them it seemed to be my unspoken challenge to cull without permission from these pages, and fashion a text according to a pattern forming in my mind emulating a legacy as enduring as the sure lines, notched molding, and fine curves of an expert carpenter and as expressive as the stitched variations on a snowflake design under the fingertips of experienced quilters.

They told me to get to work.

They insisted that I fashion a legacy of my own, based on a pattern of stars nailed into the night sky of my mind. She gave me the words—verbal fragments of us—and I shaped them, painted them different colors, laid them out on the table, and placed each one on a cross beam of our mobile memoir. "You begin with the smallest and work up," I thought, aware that I was not alone doing this. It is a choreographed collaboration, and, in a long line of legacy builders going back to Hamo de Carington, we are partners. We planted pansies this way and watched Peter Pan, and even when we were on opposite sides of the room, she swaying to music while stirring her drink with a finger and me watching from the landing wide-eyed but unafraid since she was there, was *actually* there—well, even then we were on that teeter-totter, rising and falling in tandem, lonely but never alone.

I see her now, on an ottoman in front of the book shelves with a volume of the brand new *Book of Knowledge* glowing in her lap, checking something between the new Morocco bindings, filling in a gap in her life before completing a thought in a letter, and I know, when I lift down my dusty volume to understand some detail from her past, the corners of the cover crumpled and frayed and the pages yellowed now but still aglow under my lamp, that we are making this memoir together and have been since the day she announced my coming with these portentous words: "I have so much faith in our marriage and in Max now that we are trying to have a baby."

They are varied stories—black and white and ten red—ponderant and freely floating, and the wonder is in the end that they form a single, continuous thread. She wrote letters as the line of coherence in her life deteriorated, and when she stopped writing them her life came crashing down. Picking up the unraveling ends, I wove the frayed strands together, repairing them, and creating from our common tale a new, more complex whole that stretches from our past into the future. In my mind, mother and son pass under this wondrous construction that extends across the pages of our enormous gallery, the boy beaming and pointing while the mother sinks down in her swing dress, the Gimbles' bag spilling open at their feet. She puts a hand on his shoulder.

"Are you ready?" she asks.

In my bedroom I have a Madonna, a sanded glass figurine, stylized and translucent. It was my mother's, I've been told, and in the past I liked to remember that and hold it occasionally to the window, watching the colors from the various sources of light around me combine and diffuse in this vessel of glass, but it is a cold souvenir, all absence, a glazed and icy surface, refracting light rather than transmitting warmth. I prefer the two gondoliers in the paintings that hang in my stepmother's living room in Kentucky, the figures bent together and rowing toward glowing sails, each toiling separately but working toward a common goal. The hands of my collaborator in this story do not rest upon mine—I will never feel their presence as palpable again, any more than I can hear her whisper in my ear or feel her touch on my cheek. No, her hands are *in* mine, shadow pictures of birds in flight stitched into the fabric and webbing of my DNA. Her words mingle with mine as I write so that we have, at last, the conversation we need. Our two languages stitched together with quotation marks, blurred by paraphrase, and hung aloft on the hooks of my interrogations find the point of support that allows me to arrange the shattered mosaic lying neglected on the floor, and lift it into the sky.

"That is what she gave you," Barbara said, holding the half-finished manuscript in her lap as she gently nudged me toward awareness. "*This* is what you share."

I took my mother's words into my mouth like milk and fed our story.

~ ~ ~

"I seem to be in the letter writing business," my mother mentioned in her last letter to my grandmother. "Wrote 7 other letters after yours last time (about 3 days on and off). Now I hope to write two more tonight." Dated May 31, 1960, a little less than a year before she killed herself, the letter describes the mild weather on Memorial Day weekend when my dad was home and played catch with my brother and me. Mom also mentions my little league baseball game, a baby shower she will organize, bridge lessons, the Paris summit between Eisenhower and Nikita Khrushchev over the U-2 spy plane incident, the illness of a friend, and house guests from California, including Dad's relatives and family friends. It sounds as if it is written in a quiet moment stolen from a busy and successful life by someone who is a little weary at the end of a holiday. The weather had been "nice and warm," allowing for just the kind of weekend that my mother liked. "We didn't do anything special," she wrote. "We stayed home." There is only a hint of the torment she was really going through: "Max left for St. Louis last night. He will be gone even more with this job—at least for a while."

So what happens when you come to the last letter in the last shoebox? What happens when you take that letter and set it across from your last memory, along the crossbar of your mobile made out of words, and then, with shaking fingers, dangle from it another subsection, concocted from a snatch of dream or a strip of black lace extracted from the withes of a wicker basket?

What happens, then?

The whole contraption begins its mournful wave.

At midnight on the last day of January in 1957 my mother and father woke me to watch Sputnik 2 cross the dome of the sky, and I don't remember it happening at all. I do remember Sputnik 1. We were still living in our house on Caravella Lane in Nanuet, and many from the neighborhood, including my mother and I, had lined up on the dead-end street in front of our houses to see the first satellite propelled into orbit, but the memory of the second satellite is gone.

It was an anxious time internationally, causing Americans, like my mother, to have mixed feelings about the space race. "It is a shame," she wrote, that "the great event of launching a satellite into space has to be overshadowed with the fear that the Russians are a great deal ahead of us scientifically." At the dawn of the nuclear age, she lamented that the Soviets had "perfected the intercontinental missile" and wondered about the ability of America to prevail. "It makes us all realize we have been complacent." Despite these anxieties, she wrote that we were all "very excited" and that Sputnik 1 was a "spectacular sight."

Sputnik 2 caused a stir because it carried Laika, the dog, but by this time our family had a new set of anxieties to deal with. After seven years of living in Nanuet, we had moved somewhere near our new house on Warrington Road in Deerfield, Illinois. Construction had been delayed and my parents had not yet moved in, but they were checking on it daily. "This is the finishing work that makes a house a home," my mother wrote. We were living out of rented rooms at the Shoreline Lodge Motel near Buena Park, and I am sure with the move, the delay, and the new house, that this was a busy and exhausting time for my father and mother, but I must have pestered my parents to let me see Sputnik 2 and they relented. "Steve has been so interested in the satellite that we promised him we would wake him if it did orbit."

In my imagination they both wake me, my mother nudging me quietly while shushing me so as not to disturb my brother, my father standing behind her holding my coat. I rub my eyes awake and see their faces glowing in the half-light of the room, my dad waving us toward the bedroom door. Outside it is cold—this is February, north of Chicago—but it must have been clear. The three of us walk into a grassy clearing away from trees and train our eyes on the evening sky.

Dad lights a cigarette for my mother and then for himself, the glow from the match illuminating their faces against the night sky for a moment like two crescent moons. He shakes out the match and takes a long draw letting the smoke out slowly. My mother fiddles with her cigarette before taking a quick puff, pulling her coat around her. We wait in the cold briefly, me standing between them, my mother holding me against her for warmth.

Suddenly, it appears. "Over there" my dad says, squinting from the smoke, and we turn facing east. The tree line forms a black horizon and above it the Milky Way shimmers in the chilly air.

Dad kneels down pointing up for me to see, the cigarette at the tips of his fingers tracing the arc against the sky. My mother sees it too and, putting an arm on my shoulder, leans forward to be sure that I have found it. I follow the glow of my dad's cigarette ash to the spot among the stars and locate it at last, not the satellite itself, which is too small, but the casing, a tiny oblong of light, tumbling silently across the constellations nailed into the night sky. It flip-flops in a regular rhythm, like a heartbeat, without glittering, and, despite its size, glows with a white-bright incandescence. In her letters my mother calls this satellite "Muttnik," a phrase in the press at the time because of the dog inside, but it is hard to think of a dog, or anything else, living in this slug of pure light.

I cannot imagine that night sky now without creating metaphors from the time three years later that I hid under the stairs and looked at the nails driven into the treads overhead, that coffin-lid of stars that still haunts me. Thinking of it now, the other memories come flooding back as well. Of me at the top of the stairs watching my mother crying at the kitchen table while my dad stands off to the side. Of me stepping out of my bedroom to watch my mother with her back to me singing "Fever" all alone. No, those thoughts—those precious and horrible clues—don't go away, but they also don't erase that night, lost to memory but captured in a letter that I almost didn't read, when my parents and I, somewhere in Illinois stood in a darkened field together and looked into the heavens.

I picture the tableau now like some illustration out of *The Book of Knowledge*, with me standing in my coat and flanked by my parents, my dad pointing and my mother with an arm around me, while the three of us gaze into the night sky with wonder.

"This is," my mother wrote, "a fabulous age."

203

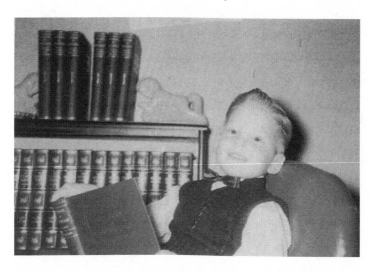

Visit the website for Steven Harvey to learn more about the author and to see other photographs mentioned in the text.

www.steven-harvey-author.com

The Book of Knowledge and Wonder

Acknowledgements

I have come to learn the hard way that books are not written in isolation. They are the fruits of a literary community, and I am grateful to have found one in those who helped me create this book. I want to thank the editors of the following magazines where sections of this work first appeared: *River Teeth, Southern Review, Fourth Genre, Ascent,* and *Best American Essays 2013.* I also want to thank readers who helped me at various stages of the writing: Robert Root, Tom Larson, Enid Shomer, Jill Christman, Kathy Winograd, Cheryl Strayed, Judith Kitchen, and Sandra Swinburne. I am grateful to the faculty and students in the Young Harris College English and Creative Writing programs for all of their help over the years, and I want to thank Steve Haven, Sarah Wells, and the faculty and students of the Ashland University MFA in creative writing, my literary home, who heard this book being born in readings and workshop discussions. Above all, I want to thank Joe Mackall who told me "you need to write this book" and saw promise in its early stages; he is simply the best friend a writer could ever have. Finally I want to thank my wife, Barbara, whose kindness to my grandmother is the most likely reason that I got my mother's letters in the end and whose love buoyed me during some dark and obsessive days as I wrote and rewrote this book.

The Book of Knowledge and Wonder

Steven Harvey is the author of three books of personal essays: *A Geometry of Lilies*, *Lost in Translation*, and *Bound for Shady Grove*. He is a professor emeritus of English and creative writing at Young Harris College and a member of the nonfiction faculty in the Ashland University MFA program in creative writing. He lives in the north Georgia mountains where he writes and sings and plays banjo, guitar, and ukulele with the musical group Butternut Creek and Friends. He is also the hardly humble creator of The Humble Essayist, a site on-line for promoting personal essays and reflective memoirs. You can learn more about Steve and his work at his web site: www.the-humble-essayist.com.

OVENBIRD

Judith Kitchen's Ovenbird Books promotes innovative, imaginative, experimental works of creative nonfiction.

Ovenbird Books
The Circus Train by Judith Kitchen

Judith Kitchen Select:
The Last Good Obsession by Sandra Swinburne
Dear Boy: An Epistolary Memoir by Heather Weber
The Slow Farm by Tarn Wilson
The Book of Knowledge and Wonder by Steven Harvey
Objects in the Mirror Are Closer Than They Appear
   by Kate Carroll de Gutes

www: ovenbirdbooks.org

53880785R00134

Made in the USA
Charleston, SC
20 March 2016